Swimming Through History

The Cleveland Pools, Bath

Linda Watts
For the Cleveland Pools Trust

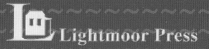
Lightmoor Press

Aerial View of the Cleveland Pools showing the upper pool and the Hampton Row houses.

Contents

Published by LIGHTMOOR PRESS
© Lightmoor Press, Linda Watts & The Cleveland Pools Trust 2022
Designed by Jess Taylor & Neil Parkhouse

British Library Cataloguing-in-Publication Data. A catalogue record for this book is available from the British Library
ISBN: 9781915069 02 3

BLACK DWARF LIGHTMOOR PUBLICATIONS LTD
Unit 144B, Lydney Trading Estate, Harbour Road, Lydney, Gloucestershire GL15 4EJ
www.lightmoor.co.uk
Lightmoor Press is an imprint of Black Dwarf Lightmoor Publications Ltd

Printed in Poland
www.lfbookservices.co.uk

Introduction

The Cleveland Pools are a truly unique survivor, being by far the oldest existing open-air swimming pool in the UK and probably the oldest in Europe. Yet their history has not been fully elaborated and for many supporters they are a 'hidden treasure', in a city whose spa waters are renowned across the world.

In common with the other researchers who have contributed to this history, my interest was piqued as soon as I viewed the crescent of the original Georgian changing rooms, still standing in their curve facing the main pool, the shape of the pool itself being substantially as it was in the Regency period. Just as the architects remarked in 2012: *'Whether intended or not by the original design, this direction of the gaze to the reflective waters generates an aura of timelessness, even mystery, that has captivated so many supporters of the restoration initiative.'*

Thanks to specialists with expertise in building conservation and archaeology, we now understand which materials were used in the construction of the mini-crescent and how the main pool itself functioned in 1817, when the first bathers took their plunge. The design of the original structures is largely visible to any interested observer.

This book sets out to offer an understanding of the social history behind the use of the Pools, from their inception as a river-fed Pleasure Baths to the large-scale public use of the Cleveland Baths, as they were known, in the 20th century, and finally the restoration campaign in the early decades of the 21st century. Through research, the depiction of the day-to-day use of the Pools has emerged, in the context of their relationship to the social history of the city of Bath and the history of swimming in this country.

This social history is powerful in that for many thousands of relatively older people in Bath and the surrounding area, the Pools represent a site where they swam and relaxed with friends or family, so it remains within the collective memory and family history. At the same time, for visitors to Bath, the Pools' history is fascinating in the context of the World Heritage city, complementing the celebrated features of the built landscape and adding to the theme of bathing that is represented by the Roman Baths and the Bath Spa.

The content of this book reflects appropriately the contribution of many of the Pools' supporters, through substantial historical research which has been a collective feat of detection, drafting and editing. History is brought to life in the chapters that are set in a timescale within living memory, as the recollections of some of those who spent time in their youth at the Pools are included, with their assent. Primary research sources have been located most substantially at the Bath Record Office and in the archive editions of the *Bath Chronicle*.

The final pages of this history recap on the fifteen-year restoration campaign to bring back the Pools for swimming. Again, the summary of the prolonged but determined campaign and restoration effort incorporates insights from some of those who were involved. This book is being published when the restoration work has started on site, despite the constraints and challenges associated with the Covid pandemic.

The pandemic has also impacted on further physical access to a very few original or primary research sources. In any event, historic research of this kind is necessarily a work in progress. Nonetheless, this history of the Cleveland Pools is underpinned by extensive in-depth research carried out over many years, and the significant volume of accrued research informs the text. The Cleveland Pools Trust is developing a Historic Archive of written sources, images and artefacts that will be a resource for those who continue to explore the rich history of this most extraordinary heritage survivor.

Linda Watts
Research Adviser, Cleveland Pools Trust
February 2022

Mum and child at Heritage Open Day, 2015. COURTESY OF BEATA COSGROVE PHOTOGRAPHY

Chapter 1

Georgian Speculation and Regency Pleasures

'... the dawn of the 19th century and the new fashion for sea bathing spelled the end of the city's period of greatness.'[1]

This observation gives an indication of the declining public popularity of the city of Bath in the late Regency period. There were major impacts for the spa, the associated city business interests and, more widely, the developing middle classes. These challenges were compounded by the economic turbulence created by the Napoleonic Wars (1803–15). This first chapter explores aspects of the social, economic and cultural context of the period preceding the initiative that created the Pleasure Baths on the River Avon.

The Benefits of Bathing

The late 18th century saw medical opinion in England tending to emphasise the benefits of sea bathing and cold-water bathing rather than spa bathing in warm mineral waters – the latter was the focus of visitors to Bath for much of the 18th century. Physicians considered that cold-water bathing was particularly helpful for chronic medical conditions such as rheumatism and skin conditions.[2] More particularly: *'Many Persons experienced the benefit of these Cold Baths in Rheumatisms, and they found relief of Pains, and a great Strength of their Limbs, and Vigor of Spirit to follow upon the use of Bathing; so that in these Instances there can be no doubt of its safety and usefulness.'*[3]

Within a few years, Floyer's popular book, *Psychrolousia*, ran through six editions, and so fed the popularity of cold-water bathing. In the 18th century, a large number of water-based health regimes evolved. Whole towns were erected on the basis of the health-giving properties of water, most of which were located in southern England.[4] At a spa in the late 18th century, the warm-water bathing could optionally be complemented by dousing in cold water – this practice was known as 'bucketing' and was thought to promote good health. Bucketing predates hydrotherapy, or the water cure, practised throughout Britain by the 1840s.

It was the eminent cleric John Wesley's advocacy that had caused cold-water bathing to be more widely supported and practised.[5] He published *Primitive Physick or an Easy and Natural Method of Curing Most Diseases* in 1747 – more than thirty editions were subsequently issued. Wesley's summation is that:*'Cold bathing is of great advantage to health; it prevents abundance of diseases. It promotes perspiration, helps the circulation of the blood; and prevents the danger of catching cold.'*[6]

Other early influences on swimming were the existence of some published manuals showing swimming strokes and discussing the benefits of swimming: '*Boys in the country usually learn to swim with bundles of bull-rushes, and with corks where the rushes cannot readily be procured … I am sorry to add, that swimming is by no means so generally practised with us in the present day as it used to be in former times. We have several treatises on the art of swimming and diving …*'.[7]

The Compleat Swimmer (Percey, 1658) gave instructions on varying forms of breaststroke and backstroke. Percey's book drew extensively on an influential earlier work titled *De Arte Natandi* (Digby, 1587). Digby was as concerned with bathing outdoors safely as he was with demonstrating swimming strokes. He recommended swimming in relatively clean water, as opposed to ponds that had been used to bathe animals.

River Bathing

The health benefits of salt water lured the relatively wealthy leisure-seeking public towards the coast, whilst rivers, if not polluted by industry, remained a venue for bathing for a cross-section of social classes. English rivers seemed perfectly suited for swimming and perhaps this is why swimming as a sport was first established here in England.[8]

However, some negative attitudes exist to river bathing that date back a significant length of time in our social history. During early modern times, rivers were considered dangerous. If the role of water in everyday life is taken into account, this is not surprising. People needed to be in direct contact with rivers, streams and other open sources of fresh water in order to carry out their daily activities; the risk of drowning was great, making riverbanks dangerous places.[9]

Although river bathing had not diminished in popularity from the Middle Ages, it was as a form of recreation rather than perceived as a hygienic act. As the wealthier segments of London society changed their own bathing habits and more clearly associated it with health and cleanliness, their views towards the hygiene of river bathing became more negative.

There were other elements to the criticism of river bathing in the late 18th century. One of these was class attitudes. Criticism of bathing involved remarks on the inferred low class of the bathers; the negative view reflected the changing broader context of social attitudes towards class and propriety.

This trend would become more evident in England in the early 19th century, as the regulation of decency drifted from informal mechanisms to ones defined by law and enforced by officials. Exposure of the naked body had been actionable under common law since at least the 17th century but nude river bathing in particular was first banned by statutory laws such as the Thames Police Act of 1814. The Act's proponents in Parliament partly justified it by '*the want of deference in the lower classes towards the higher, which had increased so much in later years*'. It was a rise in the standards of respectability that created the pressure for the new laws.[10]

Despite the concerns regarding river bathing, larger numbers of people would have plunged into rivers simply because they had access to them. Nude river bathing was popular for men in the 18th century, although safety became an important consideration – there were regular newspaper stories of accidental drowning associated with bathing in rivers and lakes. Another specific concern in Bath was the prospective nuisance of river bathers in the proximity of new pleasure gardens on the Avon in 1798.[11]

These concerns are likely to have brought about, in 1801, the Bathwick Water Act, which prohibited nude bathing in the River Avon. This would have affected local people more than visitors to the city and local bathers are likely to have resorted to the marl pits in the Bathwick area just off the river. Marl pits are the sizeable mud- and water-filled holes left behind after marl (a mix of earth and lime used to improve soil productivity) had been excavated. Marl would have been used to improve soil in the local market gardens that were significant for fruit and vegetable supply to the city. Mud bathing would have limited attractions and consequently, the idea of a more private, relatively clean and attractive bathing facility would have taken shape.

Sea Bathing

The fashion for sea bathing in Brighton, Bognor and Scarborough in the late Regency period quite literally brought swimming into the open. For Bath residents and visitors, Weymouth and Lyme Regis were the closest sea bathing resorts. The nascent seaside industry, with its fashion and passion for bathing, caused the period to be known as 'the dipping age'. An influence on the upper-middle and upper classes would have been the Grand Tour that tended to include the Venetian island of Lido (the origin of our use of the term 'lido'). Bathing activities of this type were, of course, limited to those with sufficient resources and leisure time.

Bath – Expansion of the Town, Decline of the Spa

At the turn of the 19th century, Bath was characterised by a social life that was second only to that of London. During the Napoleonic Wars against France (1803–15), Bath had benefited as a residential focus from its inland situation away from possible hostile attack – the generalised fear of Napoleonic invasion in England at that time should not be underestimated. When peace came in 1815, the Corporation (made up of city councillors) and local businessmen hoped for prosperity but declining receipts from the spa baths showed the competition that Bath was facing from the newer spas. Cheltenham and Leamington Spa, both expanding rapidly with new towns adjacent to the old settlements, were the fashionable spas and posed a distinct challenge to Bath.[12]

In Bath, the spa baths had been very crowded and hectic, and the 'season' was noted for the appearance of itinerant rogues, vagabonds and petty criminals. In some middle class social groups, there was a reaction to what was described in a contemporary publication as *'all the wanton dalliances imaginable'*.[13]

In a wider context, the public baths of the late 18th and early 19th centuries were seen primarily as cultural facilities, not as public health services. The hot baths were seen as 'infected' by luxury, and the close association between baths and brothels was partly dissolved by an attempt at a new 'seriousness' in bathing through the use of cold baths.[14]

The very local spas in England that drew visitors from a relatively small catchment area were not affected by such a poor image. The contrast with the spa at Bath reflects the city's national notoriety and the publicity concerning the more scandalous activities at the Bath spa. Most local spas were rural, perhaps attached to an inn with a physician or apothecary available to advise. Drinking wells were paved and walled around, and sometimes canopied, and where demand warranted it, pump-rooms, ranging from primitive sheds to fully equipped long-rooms, were provided to shelter the drinkers. Bath-houses were erected over cold baths, and the sites of baths and wells were often landscaped with bushes, trees and walks, and fenced around.[15]

Middle Class Interests and Concerns

By the late 18th century Bath had become far less fashionable and glamorous than during the heyday of the spa, and the city gradually became more sedate and respectable. It was becoming a popular retirement haven for senior military officers and civil servants, especially those returning from India. The relatively transient fashionable society had moved on to Cheltenham, Leamington and Brighton. With regard to spa towns, particularly Bath: *'Settled residents were beginning to move into them, many of them leisured people of private means attracted by the economical living conditions, pleasant surroundings and many amenities of the well-developed social life. This brought changes to the old mixed, public communal life with its transient support for tradesmen, hotel-keepers and entertainers.'*[16]

Population growth in the city of Bath in the Regency period was in line with national trends but the growth of the middle classes in the city is demonstrated by census returns which show that by 1830, eighty per cent of males over twenty were artisans or running or working in businesses or retail trades.[17] There were ten times the numbers of tradespeople in the city compared with the average across the county of Somerset. The use of the term 'middle middle' class can be applied to local bankers, people owning substantial shops and businesses, people having a commission in the military services and professionally qualified people such as medics. By 1830, we need to envisage Bath as a sprawling town, no longer with a large transitory population but being a favoured permanent residence. Methodism was growing in influence and the increasing elevation of respectability as a national social ethos was to develop into the Victorian preoccupation with decency and decorum.

The growth of the middle class was demonstrated in the city by retail expansion – shopping for luxury goods was a popular pastime for those who had sufficient surplus income. Trevor Fawcett describes how by 1800, *'two short streets in the inner city alone were able to boast several jewellers, speciality shops, three circulating libraries, a lace merchant, a hairdresser and perfumier, three drapers, a dealer in scientific and optical instruments, a pastry shop and the Wedgwood shop.'* Bath became the leading showroom for goods and fashions not just from Britain but, by the turn of the century, from all over the world. This commercial quality and diversity illustrate an expanding, very skilled service sector; a number of the proprietors of these outlets for luxury goods were to subscribe to the Pleasure Baths – subscriptions for themselves or close family members.

Discourses of respectability and social regulation were becoming more dominant with, at least superficially, more rigid conventions. Clubs and more private social gatherings became more numerous, as middle class social identities developed. Borsay observed: *'Prestige for the few was protected by the creation of a series of clubs and social gatherings, what were in effect status-safe zones.'*[18]

Subscription was also a means of commercialising leisure. Clubs and societies provided a setting for sharing ideas, debating and learning. In some respects, they replaced the role of the coffee houses as sites for 'social networking'. Bath's middle class residents and visitors would have been familiar with the idea of a private subscription library or a salon-type club for music appreciation. These clubs gave a sense of exclusivity, cultural identity and belonging. Privacy was becoming a valued social asset. Membership of a subscription club could provide a notion of entitlement, of respectability in a city that had some disreputable connotations. Subscription was tantamount to signing into a club, in which the costs of entertainment were shared between the members.[19]

So, we can surmise that the first subscribers to the Pleasure Baths would have desired not only to be associated with their facilities but also for it to be known publicly that they were potentially using those relatively private and sedate facilities.

Speculative Georgian Development

Development in the city of Bath was hugely problematic due to potential flooding and other challenges, such as the steep, hilly terrain. However, the definitive setback came with the outbreak of war with France in 1793, with consequent severe economic uncertainty in England. The prolonged period of war was massively expensive, and towns and cities were required to contribute levies that caused significant financial strain. Bath's boom of the 1760s and early 1790s came to an end with the Bath bank crash of 1793, when two of the city's many banks failed or 'went broke'. The crash created chaos, with massive speculative debt, bankruptcies – including the bankruptcy of Thomas Baldwin (see below) – unfinished building work and impoverishment for those dependent on low-paid labouring wages. The scale of the economic strain of the French Revolutionary Wars (1792-1802) was enormous – in 1801 Britain was supplying 400,000 men in uniform. At the height of the war, some ten to fourteen per cent of the adult male population was deployed in the services.

After years of economic turbulence, there was to be some revival of the local economy in the period 1805-09. The availability of credit, use of bank notes rather than bullion, very large taxes, and government loans and other factors all contributed to rapid economic 'boom and bust' cycles in this period.[20]

Prior to these turbulent years and then after the 'boom and bust' years, the successful building of Bath's landmark crescents took place. The iconic crescent was a key feature of Georgian architecture in Bath. The most renowned, the Royal Crescent linked to the Circus, had been completed by John Wood the Younger in 1775, two years after the building of Lansdown Crescent, located higher on the northern slopes of the city. Eveleigh's Camden Crescent was built in 1778. Smaller in scale, Widcombe Crescent was completed by Baldwin in 1808. Even smaller, consisting of just eleven houses, Cavendish Crescent was a work of John Pinch the Elder in 1830. The Georgian city features were laid out in regular geometric shapes with elegant, classical façades constructed with Bath stone. Quarried on the southern slopes, it was a milk-white limestone, weathering to a creamy light ochre.

In addition to these notable Georgian feats of architecture, the Sydney Gardens, located in the Bathwick area, were likely to be the second-most popular pleasure gardens in the country, the first being the notorious Vauxhall Gardens in London. Sydney Gardens in Bath were laid out in the 1790s to original plans designed by Baldwin and completed by Charles Harcourt Masters. They boasted a maze (or labyrinth), a grotto, a loggia, an artificial rural scene with clockwork animated figures, numerous serpentine walks and a picturesque folly of a ruined castle. Crowds flocked to promenade, to join in country dances in 'sets' in the long-room (or ballroom) at the Sydney Tavern and to enjoy public breakfasts that were served around noon. Jane Austen, when staying locally in Sydney Place, walked in the Gardens and attended events. In 1802, Garnerin, the notable French aeronaut, took off from the Gardens in his hot air balloon and eight or nine years later, the Kennet & Avon Canal was to be cut through them.

Despite the Georgian developments, the heyday of the Bath Spa had passed by the close of the 18th century. The decline of the Spa and the influx of middle class people who wished to lead a settled life in the city led to Bath becoming far less fashionable, though the glorious architectural legacy of the Georgian period was sustained.

Bathwick – the Local Area Setting and its Key Developers

The Cleveland Baths, originally known as the Pleasure Baths, were constructed in the early 19th century adjacent to the river in Bathwick, one mile to the east of the centre of Bath. In the latter part of the 18th century, Bathwick was a small country parish with just 450 inhabitants. Notable features were the old parish church and the mill, whilst the river was crossed by ferry. However, a Bathwick Local History Society publication (2008) tells us that, by early 1800, significant change had taken place – the old village had all but been lost to Georgian development.

William Pulteney (later to become the Bath MP) had purchased Bathwick and other

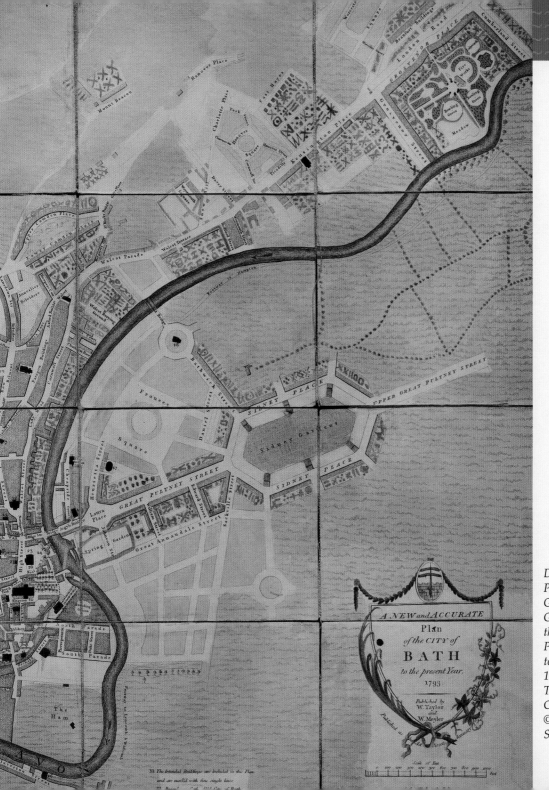

Detail of the Planned Pulteney Estate, Sydney Gardens to Grosvenor Gardens 1793. From the New and Accurate Plan of the City of Bath to the Present Year, 1793. Published by W. Taylor and W.Meyler.

*William Henry Vane,
1st Duke of Cleveland.*
COLLECTION OF TORRE
ABBEY MUSEUM, BRITISH
(ENGLISH) SCHOOL,
LICENSED BY ART UK

parishes for the sum of £12,000 in 1727. He barred any new development apart from the Spring Gardens Pleasure Resort. Bath was booming by the 1760s and Pulteney had his own vision for the area, involving extensive 'new town' development, a new bridge and a new town gaol – that was the plan that he commissioned Thomas Baldwin to develop. Although the remarkable Pulteney Bridge was completed to Robert Adam's design in 1774, the aforementioned economic uncertainty of the time prevented the fulfilment of that wider vision in Pulteney's lifetime. The critical factor was the American War of Independence (1775-83), as Pulteney was an extensive landowner in North America and the West Indies (Kilby, 2019). Henrietta Pulteney inherited the estate and was to lay the foundation stone for Laura Place and to see the building of houses on Bathwick Street with stone brought down from quarries on Bathampton Downs.

The architect Thomas Baldwin was an important person in that he was appointed as the Bath City Architect in 1775, at the age of twenty-five. That same year, during the continuing construction of the Palladian Guildhall, he was appointed City Surveyor. However, he was a controversial figure, to be challenged about speculative irregularities and investigated by his rival, John Palmer. After being declared bankrupt in 1802, Baldwin was able to recommence practising in the city but the plans for the Bathwick New Town, extending the Bathwick Estate in the form of elegant terraces surrounding Sydney Gardens and reaching a new Upper Great Pulteney Street, were never to be realised, due to extreme economic uncertainty. His works to be seen today include the portico of the Great Pump Room, the original design for the

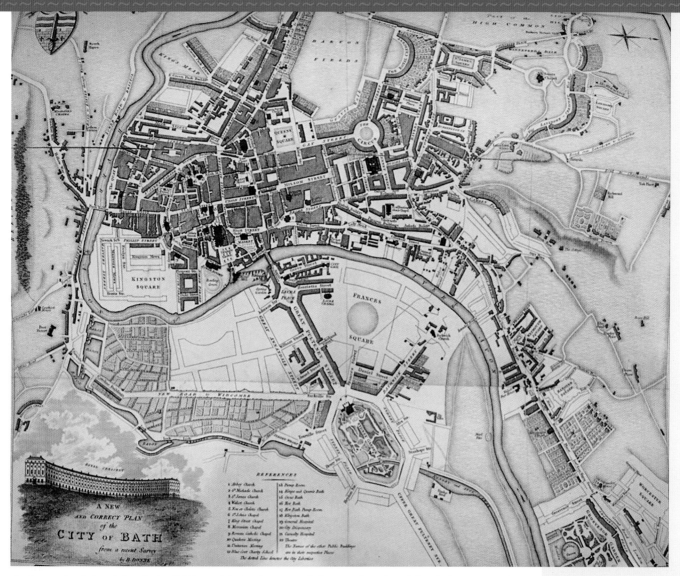

design principles. Floods in 1799 and 1800 destroyed the north side of the Pulteney Bridge as the supports were structurally too weak. Pinch rebuilt the bridge to a less ambitious design than Adam's original concept. He was to design, or contribute to the design, of the Pleasure Baths that were to become the Cleveland Pools.

William Vane, 3rd Earl of Darlington and later the 1st Duke of Cleveland, had inherited the Bathwick Estate but not through a direct line of inheritance. He successfully laid claim to the estate of the Countess of Bath, Henrietta Pulteney, who had died intestate in 1808.

Plan of Bath, 1810, by J. Donne. Courtesy of Bath Record Office: Archives & Local Studies. Note the minimal development to the east and south of the River Avon.

Sydney Tavern in Bathwick (located within Sydney Gardens, to become the Sydney Hotel and now known to visitors as the Holburne Museum), and the Cross Baths. Baldwin died in 1820 in the house that he had designed, on Great Pulteney Street.

John Pinch the Elder arrived in the city in 1793 from Callington, in Cornwall, where he had recently married. Aged twenty-four but having already designed the extensions to Babington House in Somerset, he was assistant to Baldwin and took over as city surveyor after Baldwin's bankruptcy. Pinch was to become surveyor to the Pulteney Estate and he himself was made bankrupt in 1800 but was active again as an architect/developer by 1807. John Pinch (known as the Elder, because his son John also became a Bath architect) did not build the great showpieces of Bath architecture but he did succeed in building on difficult terrain, in terms of slope and flooding risk, while maintaining good

In politics, Vane was a Whig and generally opposed to the government of the time, though he was regarded as being primarily interested in sporting matters, especially hunting and horse racing. He commissioned notable work from John Pinch the Elder as his Estate Surveyor, including St. Mary's Church and the sloped terracing with 'wave pediments' at Raby Place (named after his 'seat', Raby Castle in County Durham) that is to be seen at the foot of Bathwick Hill. Vane spent relatively little time in Bath due to responsibilities and commitments elsewhere. A consideration for him in leasing and then selling the site where the Pleasure Baths were to be built could have been the social expectation of him as being a benefactor of a certain status – thus, the expectation could be the provision of, say, a new church, new school and new leisure facility for his estate, in tandem with his speculative investments. The sale of the lease of the site enabled smaller scale prospective developers resident in the city to take on that initiative.

In summary, Bathwick prior to the building of the Pleasure Baths was an area reflecting late 18th century unfulfilled speculative vision, encompassing some challenging construction scenarios and, despite all of that, the significant attractions of the Sydney Gardens.

The Cleveland Pools Feasibility Study (Acanthus Ferguson Mann, 2006) states that: *'The 1810 Harcourt Master Plan of the city of Bath shows only fields between the Kennet & Avon Canal and the river as far west towards Bath as Bathwick Street which is lined by a number of plots and a few buildings.'* The 1818 Barratt's map shows no further development except for Hampton Row and the Cleveland Baths to the east, with the land between the Baths and Bathwick Street being laid out to market garden plots and marl pits.[21]

As R.S. Neale commented, *'What exists today in Bathwick, to be often admired as the result of the intentions of men in the past, is in fact the unintended result of the workings of the marketplace'.*[22] The development of the middle classes, including the 'high end' retail and service proprietors in the city, and the growth of social preferences for privacy, combined with positive ideas about the health benefits of cold-water bathing, all influenced the development of the Pleasure Baths, and lead us to the next chapter, an exploration of the building of the Baths on the Avon.

Chapter 2

The Building of the Pleasure Baths

'1815: The Pleasure Baths in the vicinity of Sydney Gardens were this year erected, and have proved to each succeeding one, a high source of gratification to those who delight in the healthful recreation of bathing and swimming.
The ground, where they now are, was contiguous to some marl pits (an unprofitable waste piece of land), and admirably designed to form a connection with the river, which sends a running stream constantly through the baths. They have been much impressed of late years, are nearly shut out from public view, and will soon be entirely so, by the continued growth of trees which surround them.'[1]

Mainwaring's description, as published in 1838, gives a sense of the unique characteristics of the Pleasure Baths. In this chapter we will discuss the context of the building of the Baths and will also refer to early examples of public baths in this country.

The River Avon Site

In 1809, William Bourne, a speculative developer, was granted a lease that was never formalised in the legal terms of that period. It was a form of 'gentleman's agreement' offered by William Vane, then the Earl of Darlington who was to become the 1st Duke of Cleveland, concerning the land in the Bathwick area by the river, a mile from the centre of Bath, adjacent to the marl pits. There is a record of an indenture and sale of the land by Bourne to investors Thomas Lloyd and Thomas Scott in the same year, though there is no further record of their involvement, and it may be the case that Lloyd and Scott were not able to fulfil their financial obligation to Bourne.

Bourne's original intention was indeed speculative – to build houses on the site in the context of the previously proposed 'new town' close to Sydney Gardens, to the east of the city centre. Austin and Newport were also party to the agreement – Newport was the builder who was later to construct the Baths. There is no clear evidence as to when precisely the decision was made to have baths on the site.

The Baths were located on the very eastern edge of the Bathwick Estate and would have been adjacent to the significant planned development – the very ambitious Bathwick New Town, which in the event did not proceed, due to economic uncertainty. The Bathwick New Town as originally designed by the Adams brothers (notable Neo Classical architects) would have consisted of six elegant wide streets radiating from a spacious circus hub.[2]

It could be surmised that the desire for relatively private bathing facilities led to the subscription launch for the Baths in 1815 – a short period of relative stability before further economic upheaval.

The site was on the south bank of the River Avon and separated from the river by a low raised bank, or 'bund'. The plot sloped steeply, and the lower levels of the site, including the original pool, would be susceptible to flooding. The site is likely to have been designed by John Pinch the Elder and built in 1816-17 (see below).

Overall, it would have been very secluded, on undeveloped land yet within a relatively short distance from the hubbub of the fashionable city.

The Romantic Influence

An aesthetic influence in relation to the original landscape design of the Pleasure Baths site was Romanticism – the design would have been conceived at the height of this period. The Romantic ethos is characterised by the pleasing arrangement of trees, water and other natural landscape features. The Baths' crescent of buildings, while unusual for a bathing amenity, was pleasingly simple, and would have had trees and planting to reflect the tastes of the Romantic era. The key to understanding Romanticism is that it concerns the feelings that are evoked in the onlooker – the more profound the emotional response, the more significant the landscape would be considered.

The Surrounding Area

Beyond the bank of the Avon, opposite to the Pleasure Baths, lay Grosvenor Gardens (now part of Kensington Meadows), an incomplete development designed and completed in 1792 by architect John Eveleigh. The Meadows were originally hay meadows and a flood plain, bordering the London Road, until the central area was developed by the enterprising architect. Those Gardens would potentially have been an elegant pleasure garden adjacent to a new major development – Eveleigh was building a grand, elegant terrace facing onto the London Road, now known as Grosvenor Place. The pleasure garden proposals included a secluded open-air plunge bath with changing rooms.[3] Winding paths and curvaceous shrubberies surrounded circular spaces,[4] to appeal to visitors who would have had to take out a subscription. They could take a boat trip from Eveleigh's Wharf that was in the current area of Grove Street but the serious financial difficulties arising from the war with Napoleon's armies led to the failure of the pleasure gardens scheme and it was left partially developed. It could be speculated that the idea for the open-air plunge bath with its changing rooms could have stimulated the later vision for the open-air pleasure baths on the opposite bank of the river.

Hampton Row, which runs eastwards along the perimeter of the Baths from one side of the entrance gate, was built by John Pinch the Elder in 1817-18. These terraced houses were built as artisan dwellings from ashlar limestone, a good-quality dressed stone (in common with the Pleasure Baths buildings). They were leased to tenants, including William Hall, a grocer.

In 1823, Bourne was granted a further lease on land between the Baths and Hampton Row at a ground rent of £30 per annum, with the proviso that he spend £1,200 building houses on the land. Those houses were never built. Protracted legal proceedings arising from that proviso eventually led to a legal opinion being given in November 1861 by the lawyer Mr Bricklade. He refers to the case as being the *'Duke of Cleveland's Trust Case – Cleveland Baths'*. The opinion describes how an agreement was made in 1823 between the Earl of Darlington and William Bourne, in relation to one acre in the parish of Bathwick and certain water rights, for a ground rent of £30 a year. The grant was to be made on completion of houses at a cost of £1,200, according to the plans. With verbal consent, the Earl's agents, Messrs Bayly & Savage, allowed the plan to be considerably altered. No houses were built but a large sum of money was spent on creating the Public Baths.[5]

The Regency City

The Pleasure Baths site represented a secluded, Romantic-style sanctuary for those in Regency Bath who desired that privacy and the benefits of freshwater, open-air bathing. The first record of the Baths being open for bathing is published in the *Bath Chronicle & Weekly Gazette* in 1817 (see below).

Although the middle class had developed substantially and was reflected in the first subscribers to the Baths, the majority of the population of the city was working class in terms of occupation and income. Bath's adult male population in the period 1800–20 was predominantly composed of artisans, tradesmen and unskilled labourers.[6] There would have been a continuing influx of people from rural areas seeking work or better paid work. Local forms of industry were profitable and benefiting from supplying quality goods to the well-patronised shops in Milsom Street and adjacent shopping thoroughfares.

In area, Bath was a small city and relatively wealthy or comfortably-off residents could not fail to be aware of the extent of the unsanitary, crammed hovels in what is now the Avon Street and Milk Street areas. Relative wealth existed adjacent to relative squalor. Even some of the more prestigious addresses would have been affected by difficulties arising from deficient drainage and the extent of use of coal from the Somerset Coalfield for heating through most of the year. The central areas would have been crammed with jostling carts of all sizes, contending with coaches and carriages.

Wealthy families resident in the city were more likely to have been 'nouveau riche' or mercantile in the origin of their wealth, rather than aristocratic – such wealth may have been acquired from early industrial initiatives, colonial and military service – including plantation and slave ownership – or a wide range of cultural and service activity provided for other well-heeled city dwellers. Legendary socialite and self-proclaimed 'King of Bath' Beau Nash had played his part in promoting the city to the nouveau riche in the 18th century and establishing modes of social behaviour. It can be understood that Regency Bath, in the period when bathing at the Pleasure Baths was first promoted, was a city where the developing middle classes were increasingly concerned with privacy and relaxation in Romantic-style seclusion. Their peace of mind was no doubt secured by Wellington's victory over Napoleon at Waterloo in June 1815, followed by Napoleon's surrender on 18th July. This was a welcomed end to many years of the hugely demanding financial support of expeditionary forces overseas and widespread public fears of invasion.

Early Public Baths – Design and Usage

What do we know about the design of public baths in general in the 17th and 18th centuries? One of the first private baths promoted was located in Bath Street, off Newgate Street, London, built by some Turkish merchants in about 1679. This bath was octagonal in plan and lit by a central 'oculus' (a round eye-like window) – in the manner of contemporary Ottoman *hummums*, known as Turkish baths in this country. Another bath in that period was the King's Bagnio in Long Acre, built by Sir William Jennens in 1682, with a circular bath surrounded by a continuous arcade and covered by a cupola. The baths at Portobello in Edinburgh (predating the Victorian Portobello Baths) were designed by William Sibbald.[7]

A significant pleasure bath in London that may have been an influence for the Pleasure Baths on the Avon was the Peerless Pool, as shown by the wording of this advertisement:[8]

SWIMMING and BATHING

There is discovered behind the Bowling-Green in Old-Street, near St Luke's Church, the Bathing-Waters of PEERLESS-POOL, famous in History; consisting of Chrystal Springs constantly running to Waste, which are now made into a Grand PLEASURE BATH, Where Gentlemen may without Danger learn to swim. It is 70 Feet long, and 100 broad, encompassed with a Wall, has a fine Gravel Bottom, and is in the Middle of a Grove…

Subscriptions are taken in at the Place. The whole, viz. Pleasure-Bath and Angling, Cold-Bath and Skating, at a Guinea per Annum, or Two Shillings a Time for such as bathe; and if they subscribe within fourteen Days, the Money to be allowed in the Subscription.

William Hone visited the Peerless Pool in 1826 and described a lively scene, suggesting that the bathers could be divided into two groups – those who reluctantly immersed themselves, presumably for medicinal purposes and those for whom playing in the water was pure fun:

'Trees enough remain to shade the visitor from the heat of the sun on the brink. On a summer evening it is amusing to survey the conduct of the bathers; some boldly dive, others timorous stand and then descend step by step, unwilling and slow; choice swimmers attract attention by divings and somersets, and the whole sheet of water sometimes rings with merriment.'[9]

The Peerless Pool's pleasure bath, like its counterpart in Bath, was located in an attractive open-air setting.

Watercolour of the Cleveland Pools (2016). COURTESY OF THE ARTIST, JANE RILEY

The Cleveland Baths' Design

Back in the city of Bath, John Pinch the Elder, the surveyor to the Bathwick Estate and an accomplished local architect, was on the subscription list to the Pleasure Baths but he was shown as having a free or '*gratis*' subscription in return for services and therefore is very likely to have contributed to their design. He was considered to have been Lord Darlington's preferred architect after the aristocrat inherited the Bathwick Estate.[10]

The Baths as constructed were a convenient and comfortable adaptation of swimming in the Avon, river water being diverted to flow through the original main pool, with steps for access. A filter was designed for the incoming river water and it is possible that springs came up from the base of the pool (as they still did in the 20th century), thus mixing spring water with the river water flow.

Changing rooms in the form of a crescent were created with a cottage at the centre, featuring an archway where visitors could be received. These arrangements were all purpose-designed for bathers' facilities. The main original buildings were built from unpainted dressed stone, similar to the grand crescents in the city.

The main pool was the essence of the site and the generator of the buildings and character of the site.[11] The modern pool has direct connections to the original pool form, as can be evidenced from maps dating back to the early period. The original pool was half-moon or D-shaped and fed directly from the river. There are still stone steps leading into the water for access to the pool at both ends of the 'curve', which may be the original steps that have been re-sited. There is still a raised bank between the lower main pool and the river.

The design of the mini-crescent of changing rooms and the half-moon-shaped pool reflected the design principles of the most iconic architectural features of the city of Bath. This was an ambitious and remarkably unusual idea in that the buildings of the mini-crescent were to be constructed in stone rather than in wood, hence they would be durable, unlike the riverside spas of mainland Europe.

The Ladies' Pool

At the north-west end of the crescent of changing rooms is the Ladies' Pool, approximately 15 by 18 feet in extent and consisting of an ashlar-built (dressed limestone) room. It is shielded from view by an enclosing wall. The Ladies' Pool was a secluded plunge pool for health – providing opportunity for immersion rather than for swimming. This early availability of public facilities for women's bathing is historically and culturally significant in the UK context, as one of the oldest recorded facilities specifically designed for women's bathing – in spring water, rather than spa water. Archaeological investigation[12] has indicated that the use of the Ladies' Pool dates back as far as the first substantial usage of the main pool. It is therefore an integral part of the original Georgian buildings and so is likely to have been used as a plunge pool from the very first days of the Pleasure Baths.

There is a question as to the origin of the water supply for the Ladies' Pool, as it would not have been practical for it to be fed by the river-water diversion that fed the main pool. The surmise is that this facility would have been supplied from a spring-fed reservoir located in Sydney Gardens. That reservoir was created to provide water to the residents of Bathwick, being part of what was to become known as the Duke of Cleveland's Waterworks. The development of Bathwick in the Georgian period would not have been possible without that freshwater supply. There was a substantial water flow from springs rising on Bathwick Down and Bathwick Hill, plus springs rising at lower levels.[13] The Conservation Statement prepared in 2012 for the Cleveland Pools refers to a reference dating back to 1861, that there were cast-iron pipes running under the Kennet & Avon Canal to supply the Baths.[14] It could have been the case that the Earl of Darlington authorised the allocation of spring water for the purposes of supply to the Pleasure Baths but there is no record to support that notion, though it is the most practical option.

There were dressing rooms at the higher level and those were roofed, although the pool itself was open. The original entrance was probably from the pathway to the south, on the far side, away from the main pool; the doorway to the main pool, with its window above, was a later means of entrance.

The Inception of Bathing at the Pleasure Baths

Despite the subscribers' list for the Pleasure Baths being completed in 1815, there is no evidence of bathing in them before 1817. This gives rise to the question as to why bathing had not taken place in 1816, if the building had been finished?

It could be that the building work or preparation of the site was not finished in time for the 1816 summer season. Another factor could have been the unusual weather conditions in that season, the year 1816 becoming notorious as the 'Year Without a Summer'. The eruption in 1815 of Mount Tambora, a volcano in Indonesia, the largest eruption on Earth in that historical period, caused vast quantities of ash to accumulate in the atmosphere, triggering a catastrophic change in weather patterns over the northern hemisphere. At the time there was no understanding that this event on the other side of the world had caused the ensuing climatic havoc (unlike the later eruption of Krakatoa

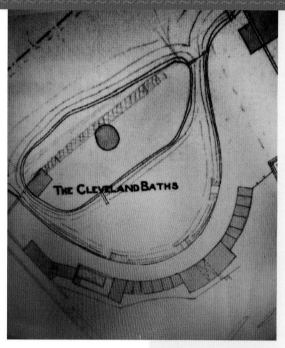

Sketch Plan of the Baths clearly showing their inflow and outflow relationship with the River Avon in the late Regency and early Victorian period.
COURTESY OF BATH RECORD OFFICE: ARCHIVES & LOCAL STUDIES

in 1883, which was communicated effectively via telegraph). Crops failed and food prices escalated in Europe and North America. Spring arrived in 1816 as expected but there was then an apparent reversal of weather patterns, with clouded skies and cold temperatures throughout the summer. The *Bath Chronicle & Weekly Gazette* carried numerous features in July and August on prayers being offered up at major congregations in Europe and the rumours circulating that the weather change presaged the end of the world.

We can only speculate that a combination of incomplete building activity and poor weather prevented bathing at the Pleasure Baths in 1816. Prospective bathers were to be alerted by this notice in the spring of the following year, 1817:

'PLEASURE BATHS. *The Proprietors of the above Undertaking respectfully inform the Subscribers and the Public in general that the Baths will be completed and open for their reception by the 11th May.*

By the arrangements of these Baths, equal accommodation is provided for those who swim and those who do not; and every attention will be paid to the convenience of the friends of this healthful and agreeable recreation. Terms may be known on application to the Baths.

14 April 1817'[15]

On 26th June 1817, the Pleasure Baths had a follow-up advertisement promoting the seasonal opening and setting out admission prices – the cost was one guinea (21 shillings) for the summer season.

Were the Baths Used for Swimming?

While men were likely to have bathed naked, the first female bathers would, by convention, have bathed separately in the Ladies' Pool and may have worn a decorous smock-like garment made of a thick coarse cotton, or linen material that covered them from head to toe. Their hair would have been covered by a loose 'mob cap'. The bathing gown would have had the distinct disadvantage of being heavy and dragging when wet, especially if the hem was weighted to promote modesty – not ideally suited to bathing, let alone swimming.

It may be misleading to discuss swimming as practised by the users of the Pleasure Baths at the Baths' inception in 1817. We can imagine that these early bathers could have performed some swimming strokes to maintain their body temperature, as Orme suggests. Breast stroke was the common swimming stroke in that period. There would have been some diving from a pool bank or river bank. Moreover, we can speculate that the subscribers who were the early users of the Pleasure Baths were accustomed to bathing while also enjoying conversation. Indications are that swimming was an activity that was regarded as a pursuit of youth, a desire that young people 'grew out of' before adulthood.[16]

In the Regency period, a more accurate description of the use of the pool would be immersion with relatively gentle movement that would be practised by most patrons. Even those who had experienced sea bathing would have been more used to bathing with a few strokes to keep afloat, rather than sustained swimming. A very few early reference books from previous centuries were available to enthusiasts, with drawings showing swimming strokes.

The emphasis was on the healing properties of water rather than on the well-being created by the exercise of swimming. The subsequent decades were to see a major change in the cultural view in relation to swimming as exercise that promoted both physical and psychological well-being.

The building of the Pleasure Baths, now known as the Cleveland Pools, would not have been achieved without the payment of subscriptions by eighty-five Bath residents in 1815. Those subscribers are profiled in the following chapter.

Chapter 3

The Original Subscribers in 1815

In July 1815 the subscription list for the Pleasure Baths opened, to gauge interest and to raise funds. It was announced that:

'The Public are informed, that a PIECE OF GROUND is secured near the Marl-Pits, for the purpose of forming PLEASURE BATHS, and erecting Apartments for dressing, &c. The object in view is to provide a place in connection with the River, where those who swim, and those who do not, will be alike accommodated. – As the completion of the plan will depend on the first Subscriptions, those Gentlemen who wish to encourage it are requested to insert their names, in a Book opened for the purpose, at Messrs. James Evill and Son's, and Messrs Bourne and Austin's, Market-place, and at the Kingston Pump room.'[1]

Extract from Barratts map of Bath, 1818. Note the location of the Baths by the Avon and their proximity to Sydney Gardens, to the lower left. COURTESY OF BATH RECORD OFFICE: ARCHIVES & LOCAL STUDIES

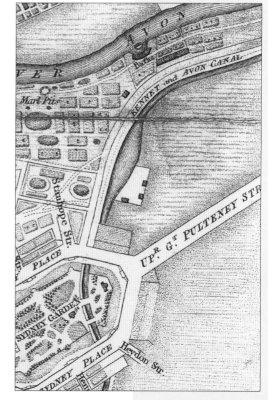

In this chapter, the context of the subscription arrangements for the Pleasure Baths is explored and the individual subscribers are listed, indicating their age and showing their occupations, where known from the relevant city directories.[2]

Non-swimmers were accommodated in the arrangements. The subscription list, totalling 85 individuals, was composed of males only. The original funding, by private subscriptions from those able to afford it, enabled the subscription list to be closed in 1815, the same year that it had been opened. Subscriptions of either one or two guineas per year were paid, with one guinea being the fee for younger men (modern equivalent is approximately £90 and £180 respectively), so the fees required a certain level of disposable income. The Baths opened on a seasonal basis from 1st May 1817.[3] In June that year, a further notice in the Weekly Chronicle stated that there were arrangements for non-subscribers to use the Baths by paying sixpence.

The Seasonal Subscription

The Pleasure Baths' subscription initiative has a clear relationship to the economic and cultural approach to subscriptions in the early 19th century: the seasonal subscription was a means of securing a regular income to help fund ongoing costs and to generate a financial return. The advantage of a subscription arrangement was that the income was accrued in advance, creating a predictable income. If numbers of people regularly attending at an identified venue could be guaranteed, then it was also possible to make arrangements with suppliers of refreshments etc.

Visitors to spas and spa towns would be accustomed to taking out seasonal subscriptions: *'Subscription was a sure way to commercialise leisure, which was applied not only to the use of drinking wells and baths but to all manner of projects, such as admission to assembly rooms, balls, concerts and pleasure gardens.'* (Hembry, 1997, p.4)

The Pleasure Baths' subscription list shows that the original subscribers were predominantly from the 'middle of the middle' class – the extent of social stratification in the city would have effectively excluded them from the organised pleasures arranged by and for the upper middle class. The developing middle class included many who could afford to allocate relatively modest amounts of money for subscriptions – subscriptions conferred a status on them and served to contribute to the definition of their place in society. Importantly, the access to others in their social group was a benefit or a privilege in that it enabled influence to be exercised and social knowledge to be gained. Such access to their peers removed the need to cultivate those of a higher social status in order to benefit from entertainments, outings or other desirable activities.

'The subscription, therefore, was primarily a tactic of the middling sort, that group whose incomes fell between approximately £50 and £400 per annum…It provided a degree of security in a period of change, enabling the small tradesman or producer to move outside the protected realm of patrician patronage without being totally at the mercy of the open market's vagaries and whims.' (McKendrick, Brewer & Plumb, 1982, pp.224–25)

Who Were the Subscribers?

The original subscribers represented the growth of middle-class professions and diverse trades in Bath and reflected those that flourished in a significant spa city. Subscribers also included individuals who had returned from serving in the British military in foreign wars or who had embarked on the early stages of a military career.

A number of members of the Bath Corporation (the formal arrangement for city governance) were involved. It can be speculated that the Mayor's subscription led his Corporation colleagues to take up the opportunity. At the time of the subscription list being launched, and then the opening of the Pleasure Baths, apothecaries were notably well represented on the Corporation – surgeon/apothecaries had marked influence in Bath. Some individual apothecaries had a keen interest in safe cold-water bathing.

It is notable that there are some family subscriptions, and that a significant proportion of the original subscribers were younger men in their late teens and twenties. That age profile is perhaps a reflection of the lack of respectable outdoor bathing facilities that could be used by younger men, especially since nude bathing in the river was prohibited by the Bathwick Water Act in 1801.

The trades represented on the original subscription list ranged from coach building to wine selling, from art frame makers and gilders to linen drapers, all with city addresses and/or shop outlets listed in the trade directories. Professions ranging from medicine to engraving and music were also represented.

Individual Profiles

Here we profile a selection of the 85 original subscribers, followed by a list of all of the remaining subscribers:

James and William Evill, James Evill Junior The Evill family were a leading firm of clock and watchmakers in Bath in the late 18th century. At least one example of their high-quality work is to be seen in Bath at No.1 Royal Crescent. The family had other business interests – William Evill had an auction warehouse on Milsom St. James Evill was born in 1762.

George and Rob Goldstone Rob Goldstone, born in 1774, was a surgeon to the Somersetshire Yeomanry, also listed as an apothecary and accoucheur (an obstetrician). He served as apothecary/surgeon to the St. James' and Abbey Poor House from 1801-04. George was born in 1800 and was also to become a surgeon - apothecary dentist, practising in Canada.

Henry Goodridge Born in 1775, Henry Goodridge was a notable Bath architect, the son of an architect (James Goodridge) who designed for the Pulteney estate, developing much of the Bathwick area in conjunction with John Pinch the Elder, who also influenced Henry's development. Henry set up his own practice in 1820. His work includes the Cleveland Bridge at Bathwick and the Corridor opposite the Guildhall. He also designed Beckford's Tower. Brunel used his services to sell shares for the Great Western Railway and to deal with major issues concerning the railway in Bath after it was completed.

Frederick Gye Born in Bath in 1780, Frederick Gye was a printer and bookseller initially with the family business. He was instrumental in the relaunch of the very popular and notorious Vauxhall Gardens, London, in 1822. Gye maintained links with the Bath area after moving to London subsequent to standing as a general election candidate for Chippenham, where he was elected unopposed in 1826. His fee for subscribing to the Pleasure Baths was gratis, to reflect his contribution to printing requirements.

Joseph Hume Spry Born in 1779, Joseph Hume Spry was a surgeon/physician who published the 'Practical Treatise on the Bath Waters' in 1822, advocating the use of spa bath waters for health benefits. He was later to practise at the Bailbrook Asylum located in Bailbrook House, which was originally established as an asylum by his uncle. Hume Spry was to become Mayor of Bath in 1830.

John Loder Born in 1788, John Loder was owner of a music warehouse, and director of the musical department at the Theatre Royal. He was a violinist of some repute, having been considered to be a child prodigy. He had played at Sydney Gardens and the New Assembly

Rooms in Bath before becoming an Associate of the Philharmonic Society and becoming well known in London. In 1817 he led the Philharmonic Society's orchestra in London for the first time. From about 1820-35 Loder was to run a business in Milsom St in the city centre, selling music and musical instruments.

George Moger Born in 1791, George Moger was a banker whose private bank was established in Union Street, Bath, in 1815. The bank was named Dore, Smith, Moger & Evans from 1815, also known as the Bath City Bank. It became Smith & Moger in 1822, then Smith, Moger & Evans in 1825, and Moger & Son in 1834. The bank's company name subsequently included the names of Moger descendants until an amalgamation in 1891.

John Parish Born in 1742, John Parish was a successful merchant in Hamburg, accumulating substantial wealth prior to living in Bath, where he was a benefactor to a number of charities.

Charles Philott (Mayor of Bath) Born in 1746, son of the Archdeacon of Bath, Charles Philott was an apothecary, later a banker and developer, who had led the challenging fundraising campaign in Bath to support the war against the French. He became Mayor of Bath for the third time in 1814-15.

John, William and Henry Stothert and George Stothert Junior George Stothert had founded an ironmongery business in Bath in 1785. George Stothert Junior was born in 1786, John Stothert in 1792, William Stothert in 1795, and Henry Stothert in 1797. By the turn of the century, the family company was making ornamental ironwork, cast-iron footbridges, agricultural machinery and even exporting to New York. By 1815 there was a separate iron foundry, and in 1836, Henry Stothert, son of the founder, set up his works in Bristol, with an eye to getting work from the Great Western Railway company making locomotive engines. George Stothert Senior was a shareholder in the Sydney Gardens enterprise. The firm became Stothert and Pitt in 1844, when Robert Pitt joined the company.

John Parish Esquire in Sydney Gardens, 1829. Published by L. Gahagan & Co, Exhibition Room Bath. COURTESY BATH IN TIME © BATH AND NORTH EAST SOMERSET COUNCIL

Other original subscribers to the Cleveland Baths were recorded[4] as being:

Austin, Thomas Born 1784; haberdasher, dealer and chapman; bankrupt in 1820.

Barratt, Joseph Born 1789; bookbinder, bookseller and proprietor of a lending library on Bond St, Bath.

Butcher, Thomas Possibly Thomas Butcher born 1774; butcher, grocer and cheese and butter factor (dealer) with premises on Burton St, Bath.

Carpenter, Robert Born 1778; accountant and auditor with premises on Upper Charles St, Bath; also a coal merchant whose duties included being Principal Clerk to the Somerset Coal Canal Company.

Cazeau, Digby Born 1771; Lieutenant in the Bath Rifle Corps[5] ; resident in Sydney Place.

Cottle, Thomas George Born 1794; surveyor of taxes for the city of Bath and the division of Bath Forum.

Coward, Noah Born 1792; wholesale and retail linen draper, previously connected with mining operations in Cornwall.

Cripps, Richard Born possibly 1800; silversmith, jeweller and watchmaker.

Cruttwell, Richard Born 1775; printer and publisher of the Bath Chronicle and Weekly Gazette. Council member from 1816-35; also had roles as a constable and a bailiff.

Cust Likely to be Sir Edward Cust or William Cust, not resident in Bath; no further information available.

Daniell, Joseph Born 1801; wine merchant and grocer.

Davies, Charles Born 1779; engraver.

Deare, James Born 1766; carver, gilder and picture frame maker; went into partnership with his father who was John Deare, a picture framer for Gainsborough.

Dutton, Thomas Born 1781; clock maker.

English, Edward Born 1781; upholder (broadly similar in meaning to upholsterer), interior designer, supplier of furnishings and auctioneer, possibly acted as agent to William Beckford.

Evans and H.B. Evans William H.B. Evans was born in 1795; attorney, possibly a partner in Cruttwell and Evans solicitors.

Falkner, Francis Born 1782; brandy, wine and spirits merchant; was to become an Alderman of Bath and partner in banking firm Falkner and Falkner.

Finden, Edward Francis Born 1791; prolific and widely acknowledged engraver with his brother William, notable for street scenes, and having an interest in engraving scenes of 'watering-holes'.

Foreman, C. Resident in Weston, Bath; no further information available.

Fuller, George & Thomas George born 1789, Thomas born 1792; the family business was coach building.

Gregory, J.N. Born 1796; accountant.

Harman, Edward Born 1775; practised as a physician in Bath from the 1830s.

Harris, Thomas G. Born 1799; brewer and carrier.

REV? W? JAY.

Engraved by T. Overton, from an Original Drawing, by T. Langdon, of Bath.

Reverend William Jay, an advocate of cold-water bathing and author of a treatise on that topic. Father of Cyrus Jay. Engraving by T. Overton dated 1817, from a drawing by T. Langdon of Bath. Published by M.T. Langdon, Milsom St. Courtesy of Bath in Time © Bath and North East Somerset Council

Hine, Henry Born 1790; tailor, apprenticed 1804.

Hobbs, Thomas Born 1781 or 1785; grocer and tea dealer at Market Place, Bath; proprietor of the Lamb Inn, Stall St, Bath.

Hooper, S. No definitive information available; possibly Solomon Hooper born 1790, nephew of a Bath barge contractor.

Hughes Likely to be Charles Hughes, born 1789; partner in coach building and harness making with Thornthwaite.

Hunt, Thomas Likely to have been born 1781; mason.

James Likely to be John James, born 1780; clock and watchmaker.

Jay, Cyrus Born 1796; attorney, son of an Evangelical preacher in Bath who advocated morning and evening exercise.

Keene, Richard Born 1782; printer in general, publisher of the Bath Journal.

Langdon, John Likely to have been born 1780; shoemaker.

Lycett, John Born 1804; surgeon and general practitioner.

Marsh, T. Born 1780; silk mercer.

Marshall Bouchier, Reverend William Born 1779; curate of the Abbey Church; in 1837, the consecration of St. Michael's Church noted Rev. W. Marshall as performing the service.

Mayhew, F. Frederick Scotton Mayhew, born 1765; apothecary.

Meyler, T. Thomas Salway Meyler, born 1782; printer and bookseller; full partner in the family printing and bookselling business from 1808.

Moore, Charles Captain, born 1788.

Mulligan, Peter & Thomas Thomas born 1791; silk mercer.

Niant Likely to have been born in France in the 1780s; no further information available.

Ninis, Richard Resident at New Bond St, Bath; no definitive information available.

Peacock, James Born 1770; grocer and tea dealer.

Penn, N. Born 1791; schoolmaster.

Pinch, John (the Elder) Architect and builder; fee was gratis to reflect service provided in design of the Baths.

Price, R. Linen draper.

Sainsbury and Sainsbury J. John Sainsbury, likely to have been born 1791. Plasterers & Tilers

Salmon, T. Possibly Thomas Salmon born 1789; Salmon's was a waggon carrier company.

Sharland, Abdiel Born 1777; tailor and woollen draper.

Shaw, George Born 1788; linen draper and alderman.

Smith, W. Born 1790; carver and gilder.

Stroud, John Born 1788; wine merchant.

Sturges, John Born 1791; accountant, auditor and bail commissioner.

Thornhill, Richard Badham Born 1760; captain with a role in the local military; author of *The Shooting Directory* (London: Longman, Hurst, Rees & Orme, 1804).

Thornthwaite, M., T. & C. Coach builders and harness makers.

Titley, Jacob Born 1790; cheese monger and corn factor.

Tuck Possibly James Tuck born 1770; shopkeeper.

Tucker, E. Born 1791; grocer at Argyle St, Bath.

Wainwright, George Born 1787; woollen draper and haberdasher.

Wallis, William Born 1783; linen draper.

Whitchurch, Charles & Thomas Charles was possibly born 1796; ironmongers at Market Place, Bath.

Wilson Linen draper and hosier.

Wingate, William Born 1786; solicitor; fee for the Baths was gratis to reflect service provided in legal arrangements for the Baths; entry in list qualified by 'attorney'.

Wood, Cunningham & Smith Printers and newspaper publishers.

Social Networking

Political power in Bath was in the hands of businessmen, shopkeepers, tradesmen and commercial interests. The Mayor was among the first to subscribe to the Baths, and a range of other subscribers played roles in the stressful civic life of the city during the Napoleonic Wars. These influential roles included those concerned with maintaining social order and meting out punishment during a period characterised by dissent and demands for social justice, in a climate of concern for social stability and protection of property.

The Mayor himself received a salary, but otherwise candidates for election had to be substantial citizens, prosperous and having enough free time to commit to civic activities. A significant proportion of medics (initially apothecaries, later also surgeons) had places on the Bath Corporation, alongside bankers, booksellers, printers and 'gentlemen' of independent means (Fawcett, 2014).

We can only imagine the political and commercial discussions that took place at the Baths. Social inequality in the city was marked, with unrest being a sporadic feature. Outbreaks of cholera and other serious diseases affected the populated areas of the city, such as the Dolemeads, close to the river, that suffered the worst conditions. In the period preceding the 1832 Reform Act, the Mayor and Corporation contended with public challenge arising from frustration concerning electoral rights. That led to the Mayor dealing with the agitated crowd who were damaging the Guildhall in the centre of Bath, by 'reading the Riot Act'. The Corporation's concern for damage to the fabric of the Guildhall reflected the status of the elegant building that was designed by Baldwin and built with Bath stone between 1775 and 1778.

The Pleasure Baths provide an example of a space that could be used by men and women of the 'middle middle class' at a time when patronage, or the influence of social relationships, was a primary route into positions in local government, the military or the church. A number of the original subscribers had existing or retired officer status in the military – they may have served in the Peninsular War (1807-14). The Baths offered privacy to an identifiable group to conduct their business, and relaxation to those who wished to socialise with their peers, away from the mannered assemblies and drawing rooms of the city, in a period when they were contending with social turbulence and challenge. Porter has pointed to the way in which polite society withdrew into more segregated enclaves such as clubs or other identified groups in this period (Porter, 2000).

Who Bathed in the Baths?

Although we have record of the first subscribers, regrettably there are no records that tell us who actually used the Baths in the early years. We can surmise that a proportion of the subscribers would have attended, particularly the younger men. It is unlikely that William Vane, the Earl of Darlington, was a bather, because aristocrats preferred private pools on their land, within reach of their residence, or on the property of fellow aristocrats.

As mentioned previously, Vane was to rent the land in 1820 for a yearly rent of £30 to William Bourne, subject to Bourne spending £1,200 on erecting buildings. By the late 1820s, the Baths were in need of repair and a fresh approach. The upgrading and the fresh approach were provided by the Reverend Race Godfrey. His significant role through much of the Victorian period is examined in the next chapter.

Chapter 4

Race Godfrey's Radical Ideas

It took a man of vision, Reverend Daniel Race Godfrey, to develop and improve the Pools. From the outset, a striking aspect of the Cleveland Pools' history was the provision of women's bathing facilities. Reverend Godfrey's initiative was to restore the Ladies' Pool, which had fallen into disrepair in the 1820s, and to carry out other associated improvements. Here we explore his vision for education, which, importantly, included and promoted safe bathing provision, in a period when that type of facility was very exceptional. The chapter concludes with some observations regarding women's swimming and attitudes to cold-water bathing in the later Victorian period.

Race Godfrey and his Purchase

Reverend Race Godfrey's practical vision was that learning and exercise were both invaluable for young people and that open-air exercise benefited everyone.

Born at Walcot Parade, Bath, in 1812, Daniel Race Godfrey was named after his father who was also born in the city – Race Godfrey senior was a physician and an Anglican Minister. He was responsible for more than 30 years for the well-known Kensington Chapel.

Daniel Race Godfrey was educated at Oxford University. He was awarded the Michel Fellowship and graduated as a Doctor of Divinity, was further distinguished by being awarded First Class Honours at Oxford in 1834, and went on to be a student of the Inner Temple in 1835.[1] He ran schools in Bath and Frome, and offered regular swimming in the Cleveland Baths as part of his educational package. Race Godfrey believed in the interrelationship between physical activity and the teaching of education.

The Reverend was active in enjoying outdoor life on the river Avon, and it is likely that he bathed in the Cleveland Baths, but there is no record of that. He demonstrated his own outdoor skills in 1833 when he took part in (and won) a sculling race from the Baths to Bathampton Mill:

The Boats started from the Cleveland Pleasure Baths, and ran up to the mill at Bathampton, and notwithstanding the unsettled state of the weather, the race attracted a great many spectators…[2]

In relation to the Baths' site, we recall that an agreement had been made in 1823 between the Earl of Darlington and William Bourne with regard to one acre in the parish of Bathwick, plus certain water rights, for a ground rent of £30 a year.[3] The grant of a more formal transfer of the land was to be made on completion of houses at a cost of £1,200, according to plans. With verbal consent, the Earl's agents (Messrs Bayly and Savage) allowed the plan to be altered considerably – no houses were built.

There was a short period of ownership of the site in the mid-1820s by John Humphries. Humphries was resident in Bath, born in Somerset in 1801, later becoming a stable keeper[4] and then operating a fly-carriage for hire from Henrietta Mews.[5] It can be inferred that for Humphries, the running of the pool was just another potential business outlet. Newport, the original builder and developer of the Baths, was bankrupted in 1827, and the Baths became dilapidated.

The Baths were rented before and after their use by John Humphries to a couple, William and Elizabeth Richence. Under their administration, the Baths in 1830 were said to be a 'pool with an experienced swimmer in attendance and also a health spa, a shower, a warm bath with a complete change for water for each customer, towels provided and female attendants for the ladies'.[6] The Baths were run in conjunction with the Richences' Oxford Boats initiative, an enterprise based at Bathampton. Boats could be hired from the Baths or from the island at Bathampton. William Richence, born in Bath in 1800, became bankrupt in 1833. He had been variously a Keeper and Boatman at the Pleasure Baths, a pork butcher, a seller of ale and a boat keeper on the Avon at Bathwick.[7] It is not known why the Richences rented, rather than offering to purchase the Baths – it may have simply been due to a lack of capital that would have been needed to make the purchase.

The Baths site was offered to the Reverend Race Godfrey, who was teaching at the Grosvenor College on the opposite bank of the river Avon. He realised that the houses proposed for the site development had not been built, so he called on the agents and was told that the agreement to spend £1,200 on houses would not be an essential requirement. The Reverend then purchased Bourne's interest in the Baths, in August 1827.[8]

A complication of this purchase was that the solicitors for the Cleveland estate gave no more than a verbal assurance to Godfrey that the house-building requirement placed on Bourne in 1823 was no longer valid. In the event, this issue was called into question with significant repercussions. It would be important for Godfrey that it was clarified legally that he was not expected to pay for houses to be built on the Baths' site. Due to this legal complication, the conveyancing to Godfrey was never fulfilled, and a Chancery Court case was put into motion. The case was not to be completed until 1871 – reminiscent of the interminable case of 'Jarndyce vs Jarndyce' in Dickens' novel Bleak House.

Despite this legal complication, the Reverend's purchase introduced a period of relative stability for the Baths. He bought the lease for the Baths plus land on Cleveland Row for £350, operated the Baths for many decades, and spent £1,200 on refurbishments within the first six months – this was a proviso of the purchase and reflected the neglected state of the Pleasure Baths. In the period of the construction work, the Reverend lived at 17 Hampton Row, adjacent to the Baths' site.[9]

The Perpetual Shower Bath

In addition to the refurbishment of the spring-fed Ladies' Pool, it is likely that the upgrading of the facilities for female bathers also included the Perpetual Shower Bath. The archaeologist's report states that there is a full description in documents dating from 1861 of '*A private Bath for Ladies with a Perpetual Shower Bath enclosed by walls and two large dressing rooms*'. The Ordnance Survey map of 1886 shows the outline of the pool and what is assumed to be the Perpetual Shower Bath (also spring-fed), in the south-west corner.

How could the Perpetual Shower Bath have worked? A functional shower had been patented by William Feetham in 1767. The working arrangement was that a basin supported by a wooden framework was suspended above the bather's head – the bather stood within the framework. The basin was attached to a hand pump which could be operated by the bather or by a bath attendant. Water in the basin was released by tugging on a chain. This cyclical process could be repeated with the same water – hence the term 'perpetual shower bath'.

View of the Cleveland Pools original buildings, showing the separation from the river by a low bank. Courtesy of Alan Travers

Becoming the Cleveland Baths

Under the ownership of Race Godfrey, the Pleasure Baths were renamed the Cleveland Baths, reflecting the name of the original site owner and possibly to lend more respectability to the Baths. In 1827, the Earl of Darlington, the owner of the Baths, was created Marquess of Cleveland, a revival of the Cleveland title held by his ancestors. In 1831 he was to be a bearer of the third sword at the coronation of William IV, and two years later he became the Duke of Cleveland. It is therefore likely that the Pleasure Baths were named as the Cleveland Baths either in 1827 or in 1833.

A potential advantage for the Baths was the opening of the Cleveland Bridge in 1827, finally linking Walcot with Bathwick by road, on the route of the ferry crossing that dated back to the Romans. It was designed by Henry Goodridge, one of the first subscribers of the Cleveland Pleasure Baths, a notable Bath architect. The bridge was named in the year that the landowner, the Marquess of Cleveland, claimed that title. The bridge opening made it feasible that the Bath to Warminster Road (now the A36) was constructed in 1833 with some associated development. The completion of the Pulteney Bridge in 1836 created a further bridge crossing between Bath city and Bathwick.

The Kennet & Avon Canal in the area of Sydney Gardens. iStock.com/Roger Mechan

During the 1830s, a Baths subscription scheme continued, as evidenced by a local press feature about a young subscriber who had ambitions to become a lawyer and failing to secure the necessary patronage, tragically committed suicide at the Baths in 1836.[10] Another drowning, also possibly a suicide at the Baths, was reported in the same newspaper on 13th August 1840.

In 1842 the pool at the Baths was promoted as now being clean. The context was that the springs feeding the pool by emerging through the pool base and mixing with the river water had been interrupted by the installation of the Great Western Railway line through nearby Sydney Gardens, part of the continuous route between Paddington and Bridgewater. Great crowds attended to observe the awe-inspiring and extremely risky construction of the Box Tunnel, close to Bath. The GWR engineering challenge and achievement included the canal having to be moved, to accommodate the path of the railway. It was observed that '*the workmen have made great progress in the necessary excavations for turning the course of the canal immediately opposite the Cleveland Baths.*'[11]

'Dr Godfrey's College'

Race Godfrey married Maria Ward in 1839. She was a daughter of Samuel Ward, a successful salt merchant and corn factor. At the time of his marriage it was noted that the Reverend was the Senior Classical Master at Grosvenor College, off London Road, in Bath.[12] The College, established in 1837 in union with King's College, was the central prominent structure in Grosvenor Place, the 'serpentine' Georgian terrace built by John Eveleigh in 1790. The College record in the 1841 Census lists 32 resident students plus the family and servants – a total of 80 residents. The Reverend Daniel Race Godfrey was then recorded as being the Principal of Grosvenor College and the Minister of the Magdalen Chapel in Holloway, Bath.

The next significant step in Race Godfrey's vocational career was becoming the Principal and Head Master of the College (generally known as Dr Godfrey's College) in 1844, with access to the river Avon, opposite the Cleveland Baths. This gave him the authority and influence to make maximum use of his purchase of the Baths, fulfilling his belief in the value of outdoor exercise for his boarding school pupils.

The college buildings had previously been a hotel with fourteen acres of grounds, the imposing porticoed entrance leading into the main school, with residences for Race Godfrey and his father in the buildings on either side. The school's facilities included mention of exclusive use of the Baths in the summer months and four rowing boats, so no doubt pupils rowed across to enjoy the Baths. There is a paved area on the opposite bank to the Baths that may have constituted a landing slip. The Reverend's son, also named Daniel, was born in 1845 – he was to grow up to take over running the school.

The school's exclusivity primarily operated on the social level – pupils had to be the 'sons of noblemen and gentlemen', registered prior to admittance with a patron or member of the school council. References had to be given for a pupil, thus accountability was put in place to ensure the 'selectiveness of the Establishment'. The pupils had supervised access to the Cleveland Baths, and it is likely that adult men and women had specified times when they too could access the main pool or the Ladies' Pool, on a paid basis. Supervision in that period at the Baths was provided by George Taylor, who had been a police inspector for nineteen years.

The Grosvenor Bridge was built in 1850, so the pupils from Grosvenor College would from then onwards have had the option to use this to access the Baths and the canal, too. By 1851 there were more than 50 students at the college: eight from India, eight from Ireland, one from Belgium and one from Newfoundland, plus a total of eight servants. The easier access

Relatively modern photograph of the central buildings in Grosvenor Place, Bath, that were occupied by the Grosvenor College throughout most of the 19th century. iStock. com/jaceksphotos

to the Baths and the number of prospective bathers at the College presented a more attractive opportunity to a potential new lessee when the Baths lease was due for renewal.

The 1850 Lease and the Reverend's Absence

The Baths were advertised for lease early in 1850, described as consisting of an island, baths, houses, a garden, boatshed and river frontage, there being no other public bathing place on the Avon.[13] In that year the Baths were seen as a place where people who swam in public places, and who had been brought before the magistrates for that offence, might now swim without offending public decorum. The person who took on the lease was Thomas Atyeo, born in Somerset in 1801. He was a labourer, living at Villa Cottages, Bathwick, in 1841.[14] In 1851 he is recorded as being a gardener, living at Villa Fields, Bathwick, with his wife Ann and their small children.[15] The Baths were mentioned in the local press as being under new management, with cost-effective fees. Thomas Atyeo took up this role in a year when the wider use of the Baths in the summer months was being considered.

The main issue was a question of propriety, that men were bathing in the river in view of public footpaths[16] – that was not acceptable to current standards of public decency. Another significant issue was the danger to life associated with people swimming in the river Avon. Swimming had developed as a competitive recreational activity, stimulated by the founding of the first men's swimming clubs. This was a distinct social change away from the concept of bathing being focussed on immersion. The breaststroke was adapted into the faster and more popular sidestroke by the 1840s. Races took place in rivers, often between landmarks such as bridges or weirs.

It appears that Atyeo had a minor role in running the Baths, as by the summer of 1850 his role was secondary to a committee that was formed to develop a scheme of charges that could be within reach of people on relatively low incomes. On the committee were the Mayor, the Rector of Bath and others who were concerned with meeting the needs of the poorer young people in the city. These individuals were willing to bear any loss in relation to the running of the Baths.[17] This was the first record of any consideration of a wider social benefit arising from the use of the Baths. Race Godfrey was still the owner, but it appears that he supported, or at least co-operated with, this committee with its social welfare objectives.

For a period in the 1850s, Godfrey was not the Grosvenor College principal – it was Reverend Gibsone. Godfrey had accepted a Lectureship in Divinity at Oxford University but retained close links with the College and attended prize giving events. It is speculative to question whether the Cleveland Baths was run effectively in the absence of the Reverend, but the local press referred to a Mr Sheppard from Bathampton attempting to organise a further subscription scheme – his attempt failed. The press article was primarily concerned with males bathing in the marl pits that still existed in the area of the Baths – the concern focussed on that activity being publicised and the sensitivity in the presence of ladies, indicating that it was a continuation of nude bathing that took place much earlier in the century.[18] It could be assumed that the concern with the bathing needs of poorer young people was linked to this issue of respectability, rather than the focus on widening public provision that developed later in the 19th century.

Development in the 1850s

The Cleveland swimming baths facility was developing at this time, having more to offer – between 1852 and 1861, a second, smaller pool was constructed, at a higher level on the site than the original pool. This second pool was spring-fed, being mains-fed at a later stage. This bath may have been established to make use of springs on the site, as a reference in 1871 mentions them rising in the pool. The hillside rising above the pools is well known for its many and copious springs.[19] This second pool was a more modern facility to increase

Extract from the Cotterell Survey published in 1852, showing the extent of garden plots lying west of the Cleveland Baths, with the land including the school open space, bordering the opposite bank of the Avon. COURTESY OF BATH RECORD OFFICE: ARCHIVES & LOCAL STUDIES

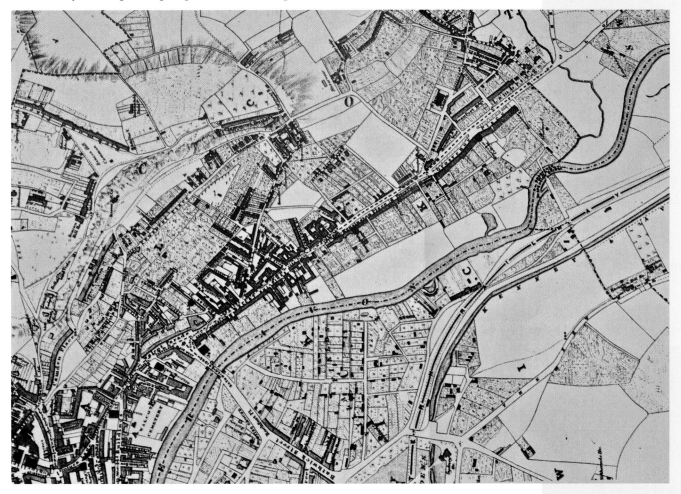

Aerial View of the Cleveland Pools, with a trip boat passing on the River Avon.
COURTESY OF CASEY RYDER

capacity for school students swimming – it was an early example of a dedicated pool for children's swimming. In the 1855 Bath Rate Book, the Reverend is recorded as being the owner of the Cleveland Baths, Cleveland Cottage and an icehouse that is shown on the Pools site on some maps. The Cotterell and Spackman map of the relevant area of Bath in 1852 shows the Grosvenor Bridge but also, intriguingly, depicts a 'natural' pool off the opposite bank of the river near to the grounds of Grosvenor College. That may be a remnant of the Grosvenor Pleasure Gardens.

The Rise of Swimming

An 1857 advertisement for Grosvenor College[20] included this promotion:

The college is beautifully situated in the suburbs of the city. The Grounds for Recreation are unrivalled, including a Gymnasium, Fives Court and Boathouse, all within a ring fence and within view of the College. The Cleveland Swimming Baths are also appropriated to the use of the pupils in the Summer Months at certain hours.

In December 1858 the Grosvenor College Prize Giving included the awarding of prizes for swimming to two seniors, named Bruere and Bunbury. Bruere was likely to have been a member of the well-to-do Bruere (or Bruiere) family who had strong colonial connections with India and lived at Somerset Place, Bath. Bunbury was William Reeves Bunbury, born in India and still having family in colonial India. Other Grosvenor College pupils included Frederick Larpent, the son of an Antwerp-based baron. Frederick was to have a career in the India Civil Service. The Garstin brothers were pupils too, both born in India while their father was an administrator. Bath had been notable from the early years of the 19th century as being *'a favourite place of retirement for military officers and former employees of the Indian Civil Service and East India Company merchants'* (Davis and Bonsall, 2006). During the prize giving speeches it was observed that:

'The Chairman, in presenting the prizes for swimming, dwelt upon the great value of physical education, upon the causes which had led him to offer the rewards and upon the great advantage which the Grosvenor boys ought to consider that they possessed, in the Cleveland Swimming Baths in the close proximity of the Avon by boat. There could not be more manly amusements.'[21]

Coaching for Bruere and Bunbury would have been given by Captain William Evans, the manager of the Cleveland Baths who took up the post earlier in 1858. His advertisement in the Bath Chronicle[22] that year aimed to attract more learners:

Mr W. EVANS, Teacher of SWIMMING and DIVING, respectfully announces that he has taken the above BATHS, and trusts, by good management and careful attention to the comfort of his Patrons, to merit their Support.

Subscription Tickets for the Season, Two Shillings and Sixpence each. Swimming and Diving Taught as usual, by Mr W. EVANS at the TEPID BATHS, Bath St.

Evans was recorded in the 1858-59 Bath Directory as being a bootmaker and teacher of swimming, living at 19 Old Orchard St, Bath, but by 1859 he was the lessee of the Cleveland Baths.[23] He was to become solely a teacher of swimming and to hold that position for nearly 30 years, being formally appointed by the Reverend to oversee the Cleveland Baths in the 1860s. (See the next chapter for further exploration of the life of the remarkable and renowned Captain Evans.)

It had taken some years to secure a suitable overseer for the Cleveland Baths who would take on the role for a long period and emphasise the teaching of swimming, rather than seeing the Baths as just one more in a succession of small commercial interests. The complication was that the Grosvenor College pupils used the Baths exclusively every school day, in the middle of the day. Race Godfrey's position as the owner was that he was fully occupied with running a boarding school and maintaining standards of academic work at the school. He therefore would not have the capacity nor the inclination to have what we would now call a 'hands on' role at the Baths.

In July 1861 the Reverend was seeking a legal conveyance of the property, formalising his purchase that took place in 1827, excluding any unknown claims from Newport the builders. In due course, the grant or conveyance of Cleveland Baths was formalised, subject to a rent of £30 from the Duke of Cleveland's trustees to Dr D.R. Godfrey – the formal document was dated 1872.

The Prospectus for the Grosvenor College in 1864-65 shows that the close links with the Cleveland Baths continued:

"The system of education' covered subjects as would be expected for such an educational establishment in that period, Religious Education, the Classics, Mathematics etc, but then the use of some thirteen acres of land for cricket etc…for the sole use of school pupils. It is stated that 'the tenant of the Cleveland Baths reserves the hour between twelve o'clock and one o'clock for the pupils of this college exclusively.'

The Baths in the 1860s

How can we envisage the Baths in this period? The Chancery Court papers of 1861 give this summary description that includes the first reference to the smaller upper pool:

'A large Bath 100 ft by 50 ft with numerous dressing rooms attached. Another large open Bath about 70 ft long paved throughout and screened by lofty ashlar walls and with a large Dressing Room. A private bath for Ladies with a Perpetual Shower Bath enclosed by walls and two large dressing rooms. The Baths are supplied with water by means of two cast iron pipes which pass under the canal. There is a substantial Messuage or Dwelling House for the tenant or Superintendent and the above is let at £70 per annum. A freestone brick cottage or Lodge has been erected at the entrance and is let at £8 per annum. An Ice House is let at £5 per annum.'[24]

Baths For Sale

By 1866, Race Godfrey had offered the Baths for sale to Bath Council. The popular, free bathing place at Darlington Wharf on the canal was thought to be unhygienic, and that was one of the considerations for councillors who were planning a town improvement package. Race Godfrey was, by then, in his late seventies, and although he was playing a part in running Grosvenor College, the Baths must have been quite a responsibility. Debates amongst councillors focussed on the impact of the change of use, from well-supervised middle-class schoolboys to potential attendance by large numbers of people on lower incomes.[25] It was thought that the residents of the Kensington area, across the river, would not at all like the sights or sounds associated with the change, especially as Councillor Jolly suggested that those who could afford to pay could use the Baths, and those who couldn't afford to pay could use the river by the Baths. The issue was left in abeyance and the purchase was not progressed. An Ordnance Survey map of the 1870s showed the supplementary small structures mentioned above and clearly indicated the separation of the main pool from the river, with a sluice on the downstream boundary between the two. There are still garden plots adjacent to both sides of the Baths' site, and the houses on Hampton Row (then named Cleveland Row) are shown with their long gardens. Seats are shown by the changing rooms and opposite the main pool, by the river bund – a low bank constructed as a barrier to the river and to contribute to landscaping. The seats would have been attractive to those watching events and competitions, with shade for audiences provided by substantial numbers of trees on the site. The river in the Bathwick area, at least, is indicated to have been a pleasant spot:

'The river god, who now disports himself in the tolerably clear stream skirted by the Bathwick meadows, must be grievously disturbed by the unpleasant odours and prospects which meet him on his way through Bath.'[26]

In 1885 the Cleveland Baths was still listed in the press under 'Public Institutions' with the College Company as lessees.[27] An important discussion took place that year at Bath Corporation's Cold Water Committee. The proposal to purchase the Cleveland Baths was discussed in the context of continuing problems with the water quality at the Darlington Wharf Bathing Place.[28] It was not possible to filter the polluted, stagnant water there. But it was very striking that over 29,000 bathers had used the Wharf Bathing Place in the previous year.

The purchase price was £600, with a ground rent of £30 in perpetuity to the Duke of Cleveland. The ground rent was nearly fully met by income from the cottage rents. An outlay would be required for repairing the cottages and improving the dressing rooms and roofs. Councillors on the committee heard that a spring that supplied the small pool was now empty and the spring entirely lost, since the construction of the Great Western Railway. A pump and small engine would be needed to supply the pool from the river. The committee took into account the costs of that equipment, and decided to try to improve the free bathing place at Darlington Wharf rather than investing in the Cleveland Baths.

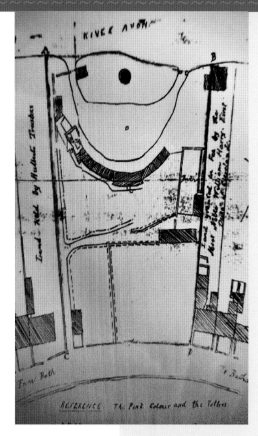

Sketch plan of the Cleveland Baths, 1872, Registry Office. Note that the Baths' relationship with the River Avon remains unchanged. COURTESY OF BATH RECORD OFFICE: ARCHIVES & LOCAL STUDIES

Brock Street – the Rival Baths

The focus of the local press shifted by 1887 to the Brock Street complex, near to the Royal Crescent, where there was a pool built in a former chapel.[29] This meant that there was a competitor for the Cleveland Baths, in relation to popular swimming display. At first, entertainments were offered that resonated with those provided by William Evans at the Cleveland Baths. A press notice announced:

'Brock St. Swimming Bath. Two grand aquatic entertainments...Programme special engagement of the world-renowned Professor Beckwith...and his daughter Miss Lizzie Beckwith, the child wonder, eight years old. Miss Amy L'Estrange...will give her unique exhibition with her lady pupils, and Professor E. Phillips will give a grand display of swimming and life-saving from drowning, and will illustrate his method of teaching swimming with his pupils.'[30]

Richard Beckwith was born in Bath in 1860, and would have been known, to an extent, in the city. The event was profiled as being a gala with racing, diving and a comic race. It was noteworthy, as this is the first local press reference to female swimmers giving such performances. In the period 1888-91 there are press features on such popular performances involving female stars, billed at Ilfracombe, Weston-super-Mare and Teignmouth, in addition to Bath.

The End of the Godfrey Era

The colourful story of Captain William Evans follows in the next chapter of this history. But what of the Reverend Race Godfrey, who promoted the use of the Baths for his pupils? He retired from his responsibilities at Grosvenor College in 1871 and moved to Stapleford Tawney, in Essex, where he died aged 84 in 1872. He had been the active proprietor of the Grosvenor College for at least 30 years. His son Daniel, born in 1812, had been committed to the College, also becoming the principal. Daniel Junior's family relocated to Stow Bedon, in Norfolk, where the Reverend had family connections and he became the Rector. He died there in 1894, aged 81. The Bath College Company, which had been formed to develop technical education in the city, purchased the Baths in 1887, selling them again to the Bath Corporation a few years later, possibly due to financial difficulties. Bath College operated from 1878-1909 in the premises on North Rd that are now the Bath Spa Hotel. Funds were bequeathed in Daniel Race Godfrey's will to the College Company. The premises at Grosvenor Place continued to be used for educational purposes until 1992, when the then Grosvenor High School ceased to operate. The benefits of the connection that the Race Godfrey family forged between secondary education and the exercise of swimming were thus sustained through financial legacies.

In 1898-99 the Cleveland Baths closed, and that closure reflected the end of private ownership. But the closure was not for a sustained period, as the Baths had established a reputation and standing with Bath residents. Although this was an era when committed swimmers and the public generally were concentrating increasingly on swimming prowess, the availability of safe bathing for everyone was a dominant consideration for the council.

Women's Swimming at Cleveland Baths

There is very little reference in research sources to segregated areas for women's cold-water bathing in the earlier half of the 19th century. We can only assume that the Ladies' Pool at the Cleveland Pools was one of the earliest examples. The Knightstone Outdoor Baths at Weston-super-Mare, the Cleveland Pool's nearest contemporary in geographical terms, opened in 1825 (Smith, 2005, p.13). It certainly does not appear to have had a separate dedicated facility for women's bathing, though there may have been times allocated for women's bathing. Well into the 19th century, swimming was viewed for the most part as a male preserve (Love, 2015, p.2).

There are currently no clues as to why the Reverend was so keen to improve and upgrade the separate Ladies' Pool immediately upon taking over the pools. It remains a mystery as to whether this was purely a business decision, to increase his potential subscribers or, more credibly, a firm commitment to the benefits of cold-water bathing for women as well as men.

One possibility that has been explored by the Cleveland Pools Trust is whether the Ladies' Pool had some use as a mikveh, or ritual bath for women of the Jewish faith. Although it would have lent itself to that purpose, being enclosed and private, there is no definitive evidence of that specific usage.

The early female bathers at the Baths were likely to have worn restrictive clothing that would have only been practical for immersion and little movement, but not active swimming. A stiff hessian-like fabric forming a loose shift from head to toe, sometimes having a weighted hem, was a characteristic bathing dress in the Regency period, preserving modesty. Dark colours had less risk of becoming translucent when wet. Later, in the Victorian period, pantaloons with short over-dresses were worn (Landreth, 2017, p.162).

The bathing clothes were certainly considered to be cumbersome, and one doctor in 1822 boldly questioned the need for them. 'I allude to the cumbrous dresses which are at present worn by those who frequent the public baths', wrote Dr Spry. *'If the patients could bathe without being encumbered with a dress at all, it would be most eligible; but if a dress must be worn, it should be as light and loose as possible; and the advantage of separate baths for men and women would greatly promote this intention'* (Byrde, 1987, pp.52-55). Dr Spry was a Bath surgeon/apothecary and one of the original subscribers to the Pleasure Baths in 1815.

In the early Victorian period, bathing costumes in the form of a knee length or longer, black dress in heavy cotton or linen were introduced for women. The emphasis was on these garments not resembling underwear, as that would have been shocking in this period. Within a few decades, women's bathing garments beame more elaborate, made from stiff fabrics in dark colours, mostly in the form of pantaloons with knee length over-dresses. White trimming at the hems provided more style. These costumes were intended to cover the body from neck to knee. Matching bathing caps were mob-cap style.

For men, there were costumes in the form of long sleeveless woollen jerseys with knee length trousers. The emphasis was on the chest not being exposed as that would not have been socially acceptable. Over time, men's costumes could be two-piece, made of knitted wool, featuring stripe trimming and allusion to nautical design influences. They were made of knitted wool. By the 1860s, nude bathing was totally banned in the UK.

Victorian society's ideals of femininity contrasting with concepts of masculinity, did not recognise or celebrate such qualities as women's physical strength and swimming prowess for most of the 19th century. Towards the end of the century, women's swimming costumes were no longer considered indecent, thus enabling them to arrange their own clubs and also take part in public galas (Cregan-Reid, 2004, p.40).

But the perennial fear of drowning and the value given to life-saving caused questions to be raised earlier in the Victorian period:

'In conclusion, a hope is expressed that our girls also will not be always deprived of a thing so desirable as the power of saving themselves from that most ordinary danger, exposure to drowning. Why should half the whole creation be debarred from doing what nature has fitted all alike to do? Every swimmer, man or woman, may be put in a position not only to secure themselves, but to rescue some other precious life also.' [31]

More widely, the debate over women's place in society grew ever louder in 19th-century England. The roles and place of both men and women in society were rigidly defined by a multitude of social conventions. The acceptance of women into areas of activity outside the home, at least for women of the middle and upper classes, was a highly contested area in English society throughout the 19th and 20th centuries. Kathleen E. McCrone has written about the place of women in the sport and leisure world of that time:

'Sport was considered essentially masculine, requiring physical and psychological attitudes and behaviour unnatural to respectable ladies, and thus beyond their proper sphere. In this as in so many other areas it was the 19th century that brought change. Women's entry into modern sport was related directly to the Victorian sporting revolution in which they demanded a share, and to the movement for women's rights, which sought women's admission into spheres previously monopolized by men.' (McCrone, 1988)

Cold-Water Bathing – Hydropathy

The Cleveland Baths benefited from the Victorian interest in water treatments, particularly cold-water bathing. The potential healing and strengthening powers of hydropathy seized the imagination of growing numbers of British practitioners and patients from the 1840s onwards, and water was used in multiple ways in therapeutic and hygienic practices. Unlike its predecessor spa medicine – with its associated frivolity and indulgence, socialising, dancing, drinking, gambling and flirting – hydropathy was 'all business'; *'its patients were to soberly abide by nature's laws, drinking and washing in nature's fluid, in deadly earnest about recovering their health'* (Marland and Adams, 2009, p.500).

That sober approach to healthy exercise was the one advocated by the Reverend Race Godfrey. His purchase of the Baths in 1827 enabled him to offer a practical facility for cold-water bathing – a radical idea for a clergyman who was to go on to have the time-consuming responsibility of managing a reputable boarding school. His appointment of Captain William Evans to run the Baths was to substantially expand the use of the Baths and to attract large crowds to popular events that were probably never envisaged by the Reverend. The next chapter explores the remarkable achievements of Captain Evans.

Chapter 5

Victorian Spectacle and the Victorian Showman

'A Mr Evans performed some extraordinary feats in diving last week, at the Cleveland Baths in Bath. First, he dived with a pair of laced boots on his fleet, and pair of Wellingtons in his hands, but returned to the surface wearing the Wellingtons, and carrying the laced boots. He afterwards dived with a jacket and a pair of trousers in his hand, dressed himself while under water, and, on returning to the surface, took a pipe filled with tobacco from his pocket, struck a light, and smoked whilst floating on his back.'[1]

These astounding feats were reported in the Devizes and Wiltshire Gazette – and in other newspapers circulating as widely as Leeds, Hereford, Oxford and Cornwall. Who was the phenomenal Mr Evans? What do we know about him? In this chapter, his achievements at the Cleveland Baths will be explored to set out a fuller picture of a man whose time there was characterised by sensational stories.

William Evan's Background

William Evans was born in Bath in 1823; his family lived at that time in Corston, beyond the western outskirts of the city. William was the only child of Susannah and Giles Evans – Giles was a gardener. In the 1851 Census William Evans can be found living with his parents in Old Orchard St, in Bath. He was listed as unmarried, and as yet no record has been found of any subsequent marriage. The Census record also states that he was the sacristan (a practical co-ordinator of church services) to the Roman Catholic Chapel.

In 1858 Evans was appointed by Reverend Race Godfrey to be in charge of the Baths, Evans stating that his priorities were good management and the comfort of the patrons.[2] This appointment meant that Captain Evans would have made decisions about the day to day running of the Baths. He would have needed to consult the Reverend about events and other attendance by the public, in addition to the priority to ensure that school pupils could use the pool safely at the designated times.

When appointed to the post at the Baths, William was titled Captain William Evans, although no record has emerged of any naval service – he may have had a relatively short period of service, though it was unlikely that he became a captain without influential connections. Evans may have simply named himself Captain in order to create a positive impression, or the title could have been a nickname, perhaps originating from his young pupils.

Spectacular Events

Even before he was appointed as the Cleveland Baths Superintendent, Evans had shown an interest in daring stunts. In 1856, for example, he was reported as demonstrating amazing leaps into the Avon after being hoisted 70 feet into the air, followed by swimming with his hands tied, to the astonishment of all who witnessed the event.[3] Evans was already experienced in teaching swimming at the tepid baths at Beau St, one of the spa baths.

When he was put in charge of the Cleveland Baths, Evans taught swimming and put on some remarkable events. It was reported that he would have himself hoisted up to a hundred feet above the pool to dive into seven feet of water wearing a tall hat 'to protect his head'! One such occasion, which took place on 28th August 1861, was described in the press[4] as Captain Evans's Great Leap. One shilling was to be charged for entry, and ginger beer and gingerbread was provided to refresh the spectators.

Many years later, an unnamed correspondent contributed insights into Evans's activities in a letter published in the local press:

Reminiscences about Mr Evans by an old Bathonian

Modern photograph of the Bathwick Boating Station with The Bathwick Boatman Restaurant on the upper level. COURTESY OF BATHWICK BOATING STATION

'He (the letter writer) said that…he recalled the swimming and diving that took place in the early 1860s at the Cleveland Pool. In the swimming matches of the day Mr Evans would have ladders placed straight up to a height of 110 feet with only a small platform bracketed to the top rails. He would close the outlet to the overflow to the river and so raise the height or depth of water to seven or eight feet or two feet above the central pillar of stone in the large bath. He would climb up the ladders and dive from that great height. He could turn in two feet of water and clear the stone pillar; also, with a sack over his head he could take it off and be free in the water. He could be tied hands and feet and free himself.

He was a believer in cold water swimming at all times of the year and would break the ice to dive in for his daily swim. There must be many who remember him.'[5]

The very entertaining Captain Evans was an expert in the art of escapology and frequently performed as a star side-attraction at the nearby boathouse regattas (Hardick, 2005). The Bath Boating Station, just 200 yards downstream from the Cleveland Baths, organised very popular regattas, and there were joint events that became increasingly popular, with bigger and bigger crowds looking on. The Boating Station sold grandstand tickets for those who could afford it. Evans would be thrown into the river 'helplessly' bound in chains and then after a long interval he would appear on the bank dressed in a change of clothes and reading a newspaper! (Hardick, 2005)

These very well-attended events should be seen in the context of the Victorian desire for entertainment. Populations in cities had radically increased due to the Industrial Revolution, and the middle class had substantially expanded, creating a market for entertainment for people who had more leisure time and available income. The early decades of the Victorian era saw the expansion of the use of rivers for pleasure boating, in addition to continued interest in swimming in relatively secluded spots.

The Captain's Eccentricity

There was a popular appetite in the mid-Victorian period for sensational displays, which could include the use of wild animals from far-off locations such as Africa. Exotic animals were kept in this period for use in popular displays, to attract crowds and to complement other attractions at shows and spectacles. The Manders' National Star Menagerie arrived in Bath in a parade on 30 August, with '*elephants, tigers, lions, camels, crocodile and offspring, baboons, gorillas and other apes, jerboas, etc.*'[6]

Captain Evans himself was well known for owning a pet baboon. It is possible that he acquired his baboon during a previous visit made to the city by the Star Menagerie. In 1869 the Captain's notoriety was compounded when he was bitten badly by his baboon (possibly the beast was in fact a mandrill) when he was transferring it to a new cage. This local press article tells the story:[7]

A Baboon Attacking a Man

'*On Friday, Mr Evans, the well known proprietor of the Cleveland Baths, was severely injured by an African Baboon belonging to him. A few days before the beast had bitten him and he then chastised it. On the afternoon of the above day, Mr Evans was about to put the animal into a new cage, and for that purpose opened the door of the old one, when immediately the ape sprung on to him, and clinging by its hind legs round his arm, commenced to bite the wrist and lower part of the arm and lacerated it very badly with its enormous tusks. Mr Evans caught up a knife which was to hand, and commenced to stab the animal, when it let go of his arm and seized him by the leg, inflicting a very dangerous wound and narrowly escaping the principal artery. The window of the room in which this took place was open, and Mr Evans having succeeded in hurling his antagonist out of the window sent for E. Evans, surgeon, who sewed his wounds, and is in a fair way of recovery. On alighting on the ground the*

William Evans with his baboon, modern sketch.
COURTESY OF THE ARTIST

baboon went to the room where it had been and was there secured. On Monday the animal (which measured two feet six inches from head to feet) was destroyed by poison. During the time it had been in Mr Evans's possession it had been quiet and docile and it is surmised that the attack was made out of revenge for the thrashing inflicted about a week before.[8]

It is notable that at the municipal reopening of the Cleveland Baths 30 years later, a number of the dignitaries present remembered their fear of 'the monkey'.

An 'Old Bathonian' living in London wrote to the local press recalling that Evans kept a collection of curios that he liked to show to boys who visited the Baths. These included '*a skeleton of a man found in a Belgian coal mine*', a stuffed tiger which was reputed to have bitten Evans,[9] and various other relics that, in the context of modern sensibilities, we would find quite gruesome.

Evans was also known outside Bath for his daring feats. He was popular at the Victoria Baths in Clifton, Bristol, where he and the resident diving master gave a series of '*wonderful diving and floating fetes in the summer of 1864*'.[10] Evans was also renowned for 'skydiving' – from every bridge on the Avon in the Bath area. His highest ambition was to dive off Brunel's Bristol Suspension Bridge (construction completed in 1864) when the tide was high. He stated that he just required a small platform, two feet square. Bristol City Council, as it was in that period, took a different view, as they considered the venture to be suicidal and had no wish to be associated with it. So the council prevented that greatest, and probably fatal, dive.

The Raleigh Company Connection

In contrast to his showmanship, Evans took a serious and organised approach to the teaching of swimming of boys at the Cleveland Baths for over 25 years. In his reminiscences, the 'Old Bathonian', writing in the Bath Chronicle and Weekly Gazette, recalled that:

'He gave me free lessons in swimming and myself and my old chum and constant companion, now Sir Frank Bowden of Raleigh Cycle fame, were constantly at the baths of an evening and both learnt under him.'[11]

Frank Bowden, who was to become the founder of Raleigh Cycles, learned to swim with William Evans at the Cleveland Baths. Bowden, the son of a Bristol manufacturer, was born in Exeter in 1848, and his maternal grandfather lived in Bath. At the time of the 1861 Census, Frank Bowden, aged thirteen, was living with a family in Bristol as a visitor while he attended school in the city. It is likely to be in that period that he encountered Captain Evans, when Evans gave displays in Bristol.

In 1872, when Bowden was just 24 years old, he made a fortune in Hong Kong. By the late 1880s, he had serious concerns about his health and took up cycling, with a view to improving his overall fitness. We can only speculate that his memories of the benefits of swimming led him to appreciate the value of recreational exercise. Bowden took out a financial interest in the manufacturers of his tricycle, and that led to the founding of the prominent Raleigh company in Nottingham. He became a proactive advocate of cycling to promote health and well-being. Bowden is just one of a large number of boys who were taught to swim by Evans at the Baths.

Modern photograph of the Holburne Museum. The building was the Bath Proprietary School in the mid-Victorian period, whose pupils swam at the Cleveland Baths. iStock.com/colin peachey

Schools' Swimming

In the second half of the 19th century in Bath, a significant proportion of the pupils of private schools, such as Grosvenor College, The Hermitage, Grovelands, Lansdown, University School, Kingswood School, Weston School and Bath Proprietary College, enrolled children born abroad, particularly in India, sent home to England while parents continued working or serving overseas. Bath Proprietary College was located from 1855 in the building that is now the Holburne Museum. These schools not only provided boarding places but also had responsibility vested in them for the overall welfare of the children in their schools. They had charge of some these 'children of the Empire' for the entire year, and so extra-curricular activities were deemed as being important by parents who were willing and able to pay for that additional provision.

One of these additional activities was tuition in swimming, which was provided at Cleveland Baths. This resulted in swimming and diving heats and races being organised every summer for different schools, including Grosvenor College. Additionally, competitions between schools were held at gala events. As well as the serious contests, there were fun races: tub races; egg dive (up to twenty eggs were thrown in the pool to be 'captured'); a 'clothes race' covering four lengths of the pool; duck hunting, to catch a live duck that was usually very elusive, diving out of sight at the last minute – the newspaper articles all say that this was very comical - and walking the greasy bowsprit, an oiled pole or spar. One exciting and notable contest was the rescue of boys who could not swim – they were thrown in at one end of the pool and other boys raced to rescue them.

In his reminiscences about Evans in the local press, Old Bathonian commented:

'He would have boys thrown in and pick them out and land them several at a time, eggs also, pick them up from the bottom of the bath. He was good at all manner of tricks and feats. He offered to dive from the Clifton Suspension Bridge but was not permitted to do so…

He gave all sorts of articles as prizes in swimming and diving competitions, and medals. He tried to buy old medallions and campaign medals from pawnbrokers and silversmiths and bring them to my father to be refaced and polished for re-engraving…

He was a believer in cold water swimming at all times of the year and would break the ice to dive in for his daily swim. There must be many who remember him. He attended St John's RC Church and robed and disrobed the priests.[12]

Evans was so well known that to the boys who swam there, the Baths were known as 'Evans's'. The opening day in each year for swimming was usually 1st May, and 'Evans was to be seen with a long pole, and at the end, in a leather sling, a struggling, shivering youngster taking his first lesson in the natatory art.'[13] (*'Natation' was a word for swimming that is no longer in use.*)

The successful blend of swimming skill development and fun that Evans organised to enthral participants and audience alike is well referenced in an 1864 press feature:[14]

Yesterday afternoon Mr Evans, the proprietor of this bathing place, afforded a numerous company a pleasing entertainment. With a view to stimulate the achievement of the very useful art of swimming, Mr Evans, who is a professor of diving, has for several summers past offered a number of prizes for the most adept at various aquatic feats…Yesterday several medals were competed for; they were well contested and the various matches offered much satisfaction to those that witnessed them. The Yeomanry Band enlivened the proceedings, in the course of which Mr Evans gave the company several specimens of his being at home in the water as well as on land. At the close of the proceedings the prizes were awarded to winners by Colonel Birch.'[15]

William Evans walking the 'greasy bowsprit', modern sketch. Courtesy of the artist

Note the reference to Evans being a 'professor of diving' – this title may well have been provided to the reporter by Evans himself. In the Victorian period, the term 'professor' was used informally, to refer to someone who was an experienced expert.

To add to the entertainment for spectators during competitions, various bands were invited to play, and notables amongst the retired military were asked to present the prizes. Evans was frequently described in the local press as being spirited and keenly interested at these events.

'The annual swimming and diving matches at Evans's Cleveland Baths, Bathwick, took place on Monday. There was a large attendance of spectators, and the band of the Sutcliffe Industrial School was present.'[16]

Silver medal awarded to Brodrick S. Warner in 1863. CLEVELAND POOLS TRUST COLLECTION

Evans involved the Sutcliffe Industrial School Band at a number of the Baths' events. The destitute boys of the Ragged School, as it had previously been named, were now being taught in premises off London Rd that had previously been used as a workhouse (the building, now used commercially, can be seen off the south side of London Rd). Improved school conditions had been enabled by financial contributions from a supporter, William Sutcliffe. In addition to the customary teaching of bootmaking, tailoring, carpentry etc., the boys benefited from art teaching provided by the Bath School of Art, and a choir was well established.

Evans's approach to inviting less advantaged children to play music at one or more of his events was not necessarily reflected in his views about the desirable social background of boys who swam at the main pool at the Cleveland Baths. His views were tested by developments in public health in the mid-Victorian period.

The social context in the city of Bath was that the bulk of the population was made up of semi-skilled and unskilled manual workers and servants, retail tradesmen, shopkeepers and skilled craftsmen – not the minority of relatively privileged families whose children attended the fee-paying schools.

The Cleveland Pools Trust has been very pleased to obtain one of the silver medals awarded to a pupil in 1863 as a prize. It is inscribed showing the name of the supervisor, Captain Evans, and the recipient, Brodrick Shipley Warner. Brodrick attended the Hermitage School that held races at the Pools. In common with Grosvenor College, St. Catherines Hermitage School took in boarders whose parents were working as colonial administrators, business managers or holding posts in military service, in colonial India. Brodrick went on to study Law and to return to his family in Trinidad.

Public Health – the Baths and Washhouses Act

The purpose of this national Act was to promote public health, especially in heavily populated towns and cities that had rapidly grown due to the Industrial Revolution. Poor sanitation was understood to contribute directly to poor health and outbreaks of a number of infectious diseases. The Act was discretionary, avoiding placing additional financial pressure on municipal authorities. It did lead to many councils constructing sizeable indoor pools, some with individual bath facilities. This was not the case in Bath. A short note from the Corporation Town Clerk in response to a letter of enquiry in April 1869 clearly indicates that the city of Bath had not implemented the discretionary Baths and Washhouses Act of 1846:

Dear Sir,

We have not yet adopted the Baths & Washhouse Act in this Borough, otherwise I should have much pleasure in sending you a copy of the Byelaws.

Yours truly,

E.J. Hayes, Town Clerk[17]

It was likely that the passing of the 1846 Act stimulated consideration of the needs of people on lower incomes in the city, especially in the context of overcrowding and diseases such as cholera sporadically breaking out in the Dolemeads and other areas near to the river. During the 1860s there were protests about the costs of clean water provision. In 1867 there is evidence that the city councillors wished that the Baths would be open for seven hours a day on six days a week:

'The Committee considered the subject of renting the Cleveland Baths, Hampton Row, and it was resolved that the Town Clerk enquire of Mr Evans the tenant, on what terms he would allow the baths to be used as a public Bathing Place for 2 until 9 o'clock p.m. daily (Sundays excepted). Resolved further that the City Engineer report to this Committee upon the practicability of keeping the Baths clear, and also as to the comparative level of the Baths and River. Resolved further that the City Surveyor ascertain the cost of erecting a shed to accommodate 50 bathers.'[18]

Evans's concerns with regard to the social status of the users of the Cleveland Baths is apparent in this record of a meeting with the Town Clerk:

'The Town Clerk reported that in accordance with the resolutions of the Committee at their last meeting he has seen Mr Evans the tenant of the Cleveland Baths who informed him that he could not allow the large Bath to be used for a public Bathing Place as it would be the means of entirely preventing Gentlemen frequenting the Baths – but that he was quite willing to allow a Bath at the back of the swimming Bath to be used for the purpose. (p.2)'[19]

The need for a low-cost, inclusive public bathing place was recognised when the bathing place at Darlington Wharf on the Kennet & Avon Canal in Bath opened in 1869, despite the canal being thronged with laden barges.

We can, therefore, speculate that the users of the Cleveland Baths still were the relatively well-off in Victorian Bath – particularly boarding-school pupils. There are no records located to date as to usage of the Baths by numbers of adult bathers. It seems likely that the Cleveland

Baths continued to serve a recreational purpose, as opposed to the new municipal baths that were springing up around the country. Those municipal baths intended to provide facilities for people both to wash and bathe in order to cleanse themselves and also to enjoy leisure and recreation. However, there were anecdotal indications that a high proportion of the population of Bath had managed to learn how to swim:

'In 1874 the annual swimming and diving matches featured the regular starter and umpire, Mr Muttlebury, who spoke to the large crowd about the need to make swimming classes compulsory. He praised a competitor named Hall – a boy aged 10 who had recently saved the life of a man at the Bathampton Weirs. He went on to observe that he could remember a time when few people in Bath could swim, and now it was difficult to find anyone who could not.'[20]

George Muttlebury's words could have had quite an impact, as he was at the time the Chief Officer of the Police Constabulary in Bath.

As noted above, the legislation enabling municipal authorities to construct swimming pools or baths was purely voluntary. Subject to certain restrictions, the boroughs and parishes might make their own bye-laws regarding the baths, and charge what they liked for superior facilities, but at least two-thirds of the baths provided had to be of the cheapest class (*Save Britain's Heritage*, 1982, p.14). The city of Bath did not have the population size associated with the drive to construct such baths, and its history as a spa venue no doubt complicated discussions about the need for a bath that was solely related to public health concerns. It was some decades before the municipal conscience in the city turned to the need for public swimming baths that were open to all.

Evans's Last Years

Swimming prowess and entertainment at the Cleveland Baths continued unabated. In July 1880 Evans organised an ambitious occasion featuring a programme of eleven events divided into races etc., for under and over eighteens, attracting a large gathering on a beautiful day. It was reported that the entries for events were so numerous that the proprietor Mr Evans had to forgo his display of swimming in a sack. Dr Tuckett acted as starter and judge – he was a surgeon and Alderman of Bath.

Prizes were desirable, including a fishing rod and a silver Albert chain (an accessory for a pocket watch). A gold pencil case was awarded to the competitor who swam the longest distance under water after diving into the pool – this was won by A. Howell, who swam the length of the pool after his dive. Duck hunting, picking up eggs from the pool, tub racing and walking the greasy bowsprit (a ship's sail pole), caused great hilarity after the serious races.

It is shocking for modern sensibilities that one 'rescue' event involved a boy described as a 'mulatto', or of mixed race, being pushed into the bath by Evans and then rescued by fully clothed competitors Howell, Keating and Hobson. Howell wore a high hat for the rescue and performed some aquatic 'gambols' while wearing it, to further entertain the crowd.[21]

The extent of the committed involvement of Bath schools in Evans's swimming competitions is shown by the Hermitage School's own event reported by the Bath Chronicle and Weekly Gazette – this would be exclusively for Hermitage School pupils rather than the events with wider involvement organised by William Evans:

'The Hermitage School Swimming Matches.

These matches were held on Tuesday at the Cleveland Baths under a cloudless sky. The prizes were stubbornly contested as will be seen from the accompanying account.

Long dive: 1, Christie; 2, F. Protheroe; 3, Elton After two attempts Christie dived the whole length of the baths, F. Protheroe making a good Junior race, four lengths of the baths…

Running dive: 1, Mathias; 2, Harrison. Mr Evans was the judge of this contest, and highly commended the winner's style of diving. Egg dive: 1, Mathias; 2, F. Protheroe. Mathias picked up 12 eggs…

Walking the greasy bowsprit: 1, Mathias; 2, Harrison. Only one very successful attempt was made. Mathias, at his first trial, nearly reached the top….

Captain Ford kindly acted starter and judge with satisfaction to all. Mr Evans, the proprietor of the baths, took great interest in the arrangements. The prizes comprised several cups and other less usual but more useful articles. They were supplied by Mr Collins, of Milsom-street.'[22]

The very generous Mr Collins is likely to have been a purveyor of fine furniture with connections by marriage to the Milsom family. Captain Ford was Charles Wilbraham Ford, retired from service and his long association with the East India Company, after fighting in the first Afghan War and other campaigns.

Weston School's own swimming competition event at the Baths featured more prizes donated by Mr Collins – writing desks, a silver goblet and a silver cup.[23]

'The annual sports at the Cleveland Baths took place in August 1882 in the presence of a fairly large number of spectators…The saving of a drowning man, which has hitherto been feature of the annual event, was not included in the programme, but quite as useful was the competition for the

The Canal near to Darlington Wharf, Bath, circa 1920. Copied from the photographer's original glass negative. Photograph taken by George Love Dafnis.
COURTESY BATH IN TIME
© BATH AND NORTH EAST SOMERSET COUNCIL

best half-hour's swim in clothes, and the diving matches were excellent training towards the rescue of drowning persons.'[24]

Skills related to lifesaving continued to be emphasised at the Cleveland Baths. Evans's initiatives in teaching swimming over such a protracted period of time were unusual and not typical of the UK as a whole. Public provision of swimming lessons was very slow to develop in this country. Civic concern focussed on the scale of reported drowning incidents. Between 1860 and 1900, the numbers of people drowned were between two and four thousand each year.

A medal was instituted by the Royal Humane Society in 1873 to recognise those who had saved an individual from drowning – the first person to be awarded the medal was Captain Matthew Webb, who was to go on to be the first person to swim the English Channel on his second attempt, in 1875 (Chaline, 2017). Webb's accomplishment caused him to become a household name and drew an eager crowd to every public bath (Sherr, 2012, p.32). In 1934 a Bathonian recollected that the redoubtable Captain Webb gave an exhibition display at the Cleveland Baths.[25]

The emphasis on lifesaving skills at the Cleveland Baths, albeit presented as a fun, competitive activity for audience enjoyment, was therefore very much related to an increasing national concern. There would have been no issue for Evans in promoting lifesaving for school boys from middle-class families in the city. The positive response from parents and schools must have helped significantly to counter the notoriety of Evans's more eccentric behaviour.

The Death of William Evans

In October 1884, Captain William Evans died at the Baths. His will was proven by Reverend John Worsley of St. John Priory – the Catholic church founded by the Benedictines on South Parade. Evans bequeathed his house at 13 Hampton Row to Charlotte and Mary Williams, also of St Johns Priory – Charlotte was the housekeeper there and her younger sister Mary was a maidservant. The net remainder of his estate was left to be divided between the Reverend and Charlotte Williams.[26] Evans is buried in the Catholic cemetery at Widcombe. His will demonstrates his links with the Catholic church that date back to the time in his youth when he served as a Sacrostan. He was remembered as attending mass every Sunday throughout the years of his demanding work at the Baths.[27]

By the time of his death, the Bath Chronicle and Weekly Gazette reported Evans as plain 'Mr'. This, however, cannot detract from his extraordinary success, not least as a teacher of the invaluable life skills of swimming and lifesaving, involving substantial numbers of school students from a range of city schools. As his regular newspaper advertisement stated, swimming was (and still is) *'that most useful art, the preserver of life and health'*.

Evans's death did not lead to the closure of the Baths – they were open in the high season, with special terms for schools in a number of subsequent years before the end of the century. In 1885, the year after Evans's death, the Cleveland Baths was still listed in the press under 'Public Institutions', with Bath College Company as lessees.[28]

Daniel Race Godfrey, who was the son of the Reverend who purchased the Baths in 1827, was by then an elderly man who was to live elsewhere in retirement. He was to leave his assets (the primary asset being Grosvenor College premises) to Bath College Company, and that is probably why the College Company took on the lease. In 1887 the Company bought the Cleveland Baths, but ownership was to last just a few years.

There was a public demand for clean water for swimming. That public demand, combined with the Race Godfrey family interest in the site ownership coming to an end, focussed the minds of councillors in Bath. A report was debated by the council, recommending the purchase for £600 of the Cleveland Baths to provide a public bathing place. There were objections to the existing free-of-charge bathing place on the canal at the Northumberland Basin by the Darlington Wharf, which was not in a good condition, owing to the difficulty of cleansing it.

Councillors were informed that '*the general public would, perhaps, scarcely realise that 20,000 baths were taken during the past year, and therefore they would see that it was a matter that very materially affected the community*.' The bathing place at Darlington Wharf was created in the late 19th century for the use of men and boys over eight years of age. Rules included the banning of bathing whilst users were intoxicated, but the rules didn't prevent the bathing place having a reputation for rowdiness. The state of the water there was reflected in its nickname of the 'mudhole'.

Some councillors opposed the report, stating that the present baths at the canal were '*not in the bad condition that they were thought to be, and that it would take a very small sum of money to make them quite fit for the purpose for which they were intende*d'. After several members had spoken for and against, a vote was taken, with the result that the amendment, to spend a small sum on cleaning the canal bathing place, was carried.[29]

In the event, a new Superintendent of the Baths was appointed to replace Evans – he was Edward Coles, a retired police sergeant. He was to be the last overseer appointed while the Baths was still in private ownership. We can see from a press account that he lived with his family in the cottage at the Baths:

"*Bathwick' writes:- Amongst the many accounts which have appeared of the damage and destruction worked by the flood, one spot appears to have been overlooked, viz, the Cleveland Baths. The custodian, his wife, and three children had a narrow escape being caught like rats in a trap so quickly did the flood come upon them on Monday night, they had barely time to get out before the flood was up to the bedroom floor…Frequenters of the bath will have some idea of the damage done when I say, the water at its highest point completely covered the roof of the dressing rooms.*'[30]

Edward Coles had been born in Bath in 1821, and after his retirement from the police service, he took up a post supervising the Free Baths at Darlington Wharf, before he was then appointed to supervise the Cleveland Baths. He continued organising annual events. King Edward School's annual swimming races were held at Cleveland Baths in 1897, though without the special entertainments characteristic of the era of Captain Evans, involving instead more conventional diving, swimming races and water polo, reflecting a shift away from the spectacle of the mid-Victorian era towards a more serious interest in swimming skills. The prize fund was contributed by Messrs Symons, Crump and Underwood, and a prize was also given by Messrs Rose and Dickinson, goldsmiths and jewellers,[31] who had a shop on Broad St.

The Baths' neighbouring area had changed very substantially. An Ordnance Survey map from the 1890s shows the substantial number of buildings occupied by the nearby Boating Station, with its boatbuilding yard. The houses built just to the east on what became known as the Bathwick Estate, on Rockcliffe Road and Forester Avenue, are clearly to be seen, with the area name of Villa Fields (no longer used in the present day) being shown.

The Context of Swimming in the Victorian Period

At the start of the 19th century, swimming had been experienced as a relatively free and unrestricted exercise, making use of rivers and natural pools, albeit at risk of drowning accidents and the hazards of mud and polluted waters. By the end of the century, though, '*to swim, one now had to own a special costume and have a place specifically designated for swimming*' (Cregan-Reid, 2004, pp.40-41). The increasing commercialisation of swimming meant that a wider variety of costumes were available though many women's bathing dresses resembled everyday ankle-length dresses. Expertise in swimming and competitive strategies became valued and publicised.

The teaching of swimming becomes more prominent in the later Victorian period, in private schools or at baths where there were entrance fees. Most people who learned to swim would have been male and in younger age groups. During the late 19th century, the roles of trainers and coaches emerged and developed, in addition to the skills of performers and competitive swimmers. The term 'professor' was more commonly used than 'coach' – thus Captain Evans was sometimes described in the press as being a 'professor of swimming'. Swimming races became common and the Amateur Swimming Association was formed. In the UK, the first amateur swimming school opened in 1875. Public concern about the importance of life saving led to a focus on life saving skills in water, as drowning in rivers and lakes was frequently reported in the press.

Breaststroke was still the predominant swimming stroke practised in this country – an adaptation was sidestroke, which increased speed of movement. Front crawl was practised in North and South America, and was very gradually introduced in this country, though there was resistance to the splashing arm strokes and the tendency for the swimmer's face to be in the water. (Chaline, 2017).

Swimming and diving feats were hugely popular spectator sports, involving high dives, escapology and other stunts. Water polo competitions and other team efforts such as synchronised swimming became very popular in this period, also drawing in spectators. Swimming became an Olympic sport for men, in the 1890s. In 1896 there were just four men's races, held in the Mediterranean Sea.

Cold water immersion and swimming was still very much advocated by medics for health reasons, though the science of the stimulation of the immune system was not yet fully understood. That emphasis on the health benefits influenced the scale of bathing in rivers and pools. Queen Victoria tried sea bathing in the 1840s at the Isle of Wight – that would have been influential for women who were able to take up the opportunity.

Other relatively early bathing pools that are still in existence were constructed in the Victorian era. The Clifton Pool in Bristol was completed in 1850, and the Pells Pool in Lewes was constructed in 1860. The Clifton Pool has some remaining heritage features that are Grade II* listed – that pool is open-air, with a poolside restaurant, and is in private ownership. The Pells Pool is an unheated, spring-fed freshwater pool, run by a community association. Swimmers from the Chippenham Baths took part in competitions at the Cleveland Baths. The Chippenham Baths were founded in 1877 on a backwater of the Avon. Detailed information on pools and lidos in England, whether they are still existing or long-demolished, is to be found in the book Liquid Assets (Smith and Inglis, 2005).

One influential factor in relation to swimming was the seaside excursion. Through the century, there was a massive increase in the scale of excursions to the seaside, especially after railway travel became more established. The seaside excursion became a feature of the lives of working-class families, after the initial period when it was only within the reach of middle-class incomes. From Bath, the train journey from the Green Park station to Weston-super-Mare on the Somerset coast became hugely popular in the season. Access to sandy beaches in the summer naturally stimulated interest in sea bathing, with the bathing machine phasing out in favour of beach huts and changing-room facilities.

But women who opted to swim informally in fresh water were liable to be arrested in the context of an offence against public decency. Margaret Nevinson, who had been a notable suffragette, remarked on this in a newspaper piece in the 1930s. She cited an example of an arrest in London in the 1880s, in a period when women fought against being debarred from using natural pools: 'We were out for the right to swim as well as the right to vote.'[32]

However, the growth of swimming clubs including women's membership was significant – by 1880, when the national Amateur Swimming Association was formed, there were over 300 clubs in regional areas in this country (Doughan and Gordon, 2006). The acceptance of the value of swimming lessons and the blossoming of swimming clubs were, by the 1890s, factors in ensuring that municipal swimming pools were seen as badges of municipal enterprise (Clarke and Critcher, 1985, p.65). The renowned Bath Dolphin Swimming Club was founded in 1899 at the Cleveland Baths, having a membership that warranted immediate demands for both indoor and outdoor swimming facilities.

The growth of wide public interest in swimming competence, together with the formation of swimming clubs, was the context for the significant discussion by Bath Corporation Councillors at the end of the 19th century, focussing again on the acquisition of the Cleveland Baths for public use for residents in Bath of all classes. The next chapter examines the implications of the fulfilment of that change of ownership.

Chapter 6

Bath Corporation – A New Baths Owner for the 20th Century

In 1900, very fortunately for future generations, Bath Corporation's Waterworks Committee formally took on the ownership of the Cleveland Baths after many years of consideration. The pools site was purchased by the Corporation from the Bath College Company for the sum of £100.

In this chapter, the implications of council ownership in the first two decades of the 20th century are explored, and Samuel Inkerman Bailey, the first Superintendent appointed under council ownership, is profiled. The contextual influences of the First World War, club swimming, lifesaving, women's swimming and other pools of this period are also examined more briefly.

Bath Corporation's Purchase of the Baths

The culmination of private ownership was indicated in 1898–99 when the Cleveland Baths had closed due to the liquidation of the owners (Bath College Company of Grosvenor Place). Bath College Company was a precursor of Bath City College. It had absorbed the legacies of Reverend Race Godfrey and his son of the same name, whose educational bequests were made over to the Company. The Baths were refurbished by the Corporation with the intention of replacing the inadequate free bathing place at Darlington Wharf on the Kennet & Avon Canal. The conditions there for bathers were problematic, as the canal would have been thronged with barges carrying coal, Bath stone, timber and foodstuffs. The wharf was the point at which the canal had been diverted to accommodate Brunel's railway.

The Waterworks Committee's view was that the outlay on the Cleveland Baths was relatively small, and if they could provide a place for boys to swim, they would at the same time be providing a setting for adults to learn to swim too. To that end they indicated that they would build a new small pool 70 by 20 feet at a cost of £510. This plan would perhaps do away with river bathing, which to some was still objectionable, even a hundred years after the Bathwick Water Act prohibited that activity. It was thought that the costs of the pool would be covered by a profit made by the Waterworks Committee in the previous year.[1]

Approximately £600 was spent on improving the main pool and creating the new smaller pool. Springs that had previously surfaced at the smaller pool were no longer in evidence.

It was assumed that the temperature of the water in the main bath would be the coldest, but tests made by Mr Gilby, the Waterworks Engineer, showed that the temperature of the water in the new smaller pool, the main bath and the river were all very similar. On the morning of the reopening of the Baths, the temperature of both pools was 53 degrees centigrade, while the river was a similar 52 degrees.[2]

Reopening Ceremony

For Bath Corporation members, their civic initiative and investment in the Baths warranted headline publicity in the local press and a high profile in the city. The Baths were ceremonially reopened on 30 April 1901[3] by the then Mayor, Mr T.B. Silcock, an architect with a practice at the Octagon Chambers. The Chairman of the Waterworks Committee, J.E. Henshaw, made an impressive speech. James Eli Henshaw, then aged 36, was passionate about promoting sports and was the Chairman of Bath Football Club, in addition to having a leading role in the upgrading and reopening of the Cleveland Baths. He was to become the next mayor. Some 27 councillors were present at the event, accompanied by the Town Clerk, the Waterworks Engineer, the Medical Officer of Health and Mr Bailey, the first Baths Superintendent to be appointed by the new owners. This was clearly a significant occasion for the Bath Corporation.

Why would the council's Waterworks Committee involve itself in such a venture when its main objective had to be the supply of clean water to the people of Bath? The Bath Chronicle and Weekly Gazette reported fully on the opening ceremonials and speculated that the Committee's interest was 'public spirited'. Reference was made to the long-held aim of providing a satisfactory bathing place for the younger citizens of Bath. Alderman Thomas Jolly, who was said to be sadly missed, had been extremely anxious that the bathing place on the canal should be superseded by something better.

One speaker at the opening ceremony rejoiced that they had acquired the pool for just £100, but Mr Alfred Moger, the city treasurer (and a descendant of one of the original Baths subscribers), had reminded them that morning, in a speech to Council, that the Waterworks Committee had outstanding major financial issues. Mr Moger said he had lively recollections of the Baths himself, and raised a laugh with his mention of the monkey that had terrified them all (he was referring to the ape that was owned by the notorious Captain Evans).[4]

The popularity of the Baths for city residents was a key consideration for councillors. They had competing interests, as they were also aiming to revive tourist interest in the Spa in the same period. Interestingly, the Corporation's allocated funds for improvements to the Cleveland Baths deliberately equalled the level of funds allocated to the Spa. Admission to the Baths was free at first – but that public benefit did not last for long, due to the financial pressures on the Corporation.

The context of the popular interest in swimming is an important factor to take into account in relation to the council's actions towards the Cleveland Baths. By the end of May 1901, 195 bathers, mainly boys, had used the pool on one day. The Corporation ensured that their new Superintendent, Samuel Inkerman Bailey, was formally responsible for keeping order at the Baths, by passing bye-laws in April 1901 that set out his duties towards the care of the premises, monitoring behaviour and specifically not allowing *'any bather to enter the river from the premises of the Bathing Places'*.[5] Councillors intended that bathers' behaviour at the Baths should be orderly and respectable, compared to their impressions of the rowdy behaviour at the canal bathing place.

Superintendent Inkerman Bailey

Given the acknowledged need to keep order at the Cleveland Baths, it can be understood that the Corporation considered that their first Superintendent should have recognised status and be able to command respect. The first resident Superintendent appointed by the Corporation was Samuel Inkerman Bailey, who had served with the Royal Navy.

Bailey's descendants who live in the Bath area have provided the Cleveland Pools Trust with key family history information. Samuel was born in Widcombe, Bath, in 1861 or 1862, and was given the second name Inkerman by his parents Joseph and Lucy to honour the memory of a great uncle who had been killed in the Crimean War Battle of Inkerman in 1854.[6] Samuel entered Navy service probably as a young teenager and then rose through the ranks. Samuel's obituary[7] refers to his first ship as being HMS Formidable. However, HMS (later TS, or Training Ship) Formidable was not in action at the time, as it was leased to the Bristol Training Ship Association and provided a base for The National Nautical School in

Photograph of Samuel Inkerman Bailey and Joanna Bailey, COURTESY OF HIS FAMILY DESCENDANTS. *Note that this is a 'melded' photograph, from two separate photographs.*

Portishead. The school was created in 1869 for destitute and neglected boys of Bristol, and although Samuel may have been living in Bath, it is quite plausible that he attended.

Samuel was entrusted with service as coxswain on the Royal yacht Victoria and Albert when it was used by Queen Victoria. He retired from the Navy with the rank of Chief Petty Officer and served in a variety of posts, eventually becoming a Petty Officer Class 1, leaving active service on 31st March 1900. His main naval trade was in gunnery. Directly he returned to his native city of Bath, he was appointed as Superintendent of the Cleveland Baths, replacing Mr Cole, who also had been a 'Navy man' (see previous chapter).

The 1901 Census on the night of 31st March shows Samuel Inkerman Bailey as living at the Free Baths Bathwick, as Superintendent and being a single man. From his obituary in the Bath Chronicle, this residence appears to have been the Free Baths on the canal, where Bailey took over as Superintendent from Mr Cole, who had been there for 29 years. The Cleveland Baths reopened later in 1901.

Samuel married Alice Joanna Clark, who was from Frome, in spring 1901, possibly after he was certain that he had been appointed to his new post at the Cleveland Baths. They raised a young family of three sons and two daughters, who were all born while he was the Baths' Superintendent. Before the First World War, the Inkerman Baileys lived at the Cleveland Baths and then moved to 4 Cleveland Place for a short while, before moving further down the road into Hampton Row, at Railway Cottages. Samuel's great-grandson Mark Eades swam at the Cleveland Baths in the 1970s – Mark and other family members have contributed photographs and documents to the Cleveland Pools heritage archives.

Samuel was commended in his presence at the reopening of the Baths in 1901. Mr Henshaw, the Chairman of the Waterworks Committee, stated in his speech that in Mr Bailey they had an excellent custodian, as for several years he was captain's coxswain on the training ship St. Vincent. The Chairman was of the opinion that the teaching of swimming was a very important duty and that he would like to see it made obligatory ('Hear, hear!' came from the assembled crowd). A few years previously, Mr Henshaw had fallen from a boat into seven or eight feet of flood water on the Lower Bristol Road and thought that he would undoubtedly have drowned had he not known how to swim. Mr Henshaw remarked that in the summer of 1900, there were close on 9,000 swimmers using the old main bath, despite the unsatisfactory conditions, and he was sure that those numbers would be exceeded in the forthcoming summer.

Tensions arose due to the popularity of the Baths. A letter to the Bath Chronicle and Weekly Gazette published in August 1901 complained about the periods of exclusive use of the Baths by the King Edward and Grosvenor schools, referring to 'the inconvenience to the public'. This usage by the schools was a continuation of their use of the Baths in the late Victorian period, but it appeared to some residents of the city to be at odds with the new spirit of public access to the pools.[8]

Club Swimming

In addition to use by individual bathers, the Corporation would have had representations from the swimming clubs – the YMCA club had been founded in 1895; the Bath Dolphin Club was founded at the Cleveland Baths four years later.[9] Both clubs were interested in having the option of a base for safe outdoor swimming. By the summer of 1902, competitive swimming was established in the Baths, with the Dolphins holding junior races in summer and autumn. In the following year, the YMCA Bath was to organise handicap races. For 25 years after its founding, the Dolphin Club used the indoor swimming facility at the New Royal Baths, an updated aspect of the Bath Spa complex. These new baths had been completed in 1870, providing a pool, plus spa treatment rooms.

The Dolphin Club also had a River Swimming Station – a base for outdoor swimmers – at the Cleveland Baths. The overview of the Club's history speculates whether the River Swimming Station existed from the Club's inception; but there are no records that provide a definitive answer to that question. The Club was using the river for distance swimming – in February 1902 it was looking for a bathing shed to facilitate river swimming, and it was proposed that this might be at the Cleveland Baths site, near the river edge. At the end of that year there was discussion at the Dolphin Club annual dinner about the provision of cold-water swimming, and it was said that it took six or eight men six weeks to pump out the Cleveland bath and to clean it. This reflected concerns about how labour-intensive it was to clean the pool.

The YMCA club was also involved with river swimming in 1902, but its interest in the Cleveland Baths is shown in its suggestions for changes to the pool, involving squaring of

Bath Dolphins Swimming Club and YMCA Swimming Club riverside access for swimming in the Avon, circa 1910. COURTESY BATH IN TIME © BATH AND NORTH EAST SOMERSET COUNCIL

the deep end, removal of steps round the pool, increasing room for the public by moving back dressing rooms, and improved lighting. The council agreed to consider these points but was concerned that they would be costly.[10]

Issues about widening the social use of the Baths continued to arise – in May 1902 there was a request from female swimmers for a reserved time for them to use the pool three times a week. They were offered one session for two hours on Tuesdays. In order to acknowledge the perceived need for modesty and privacy, it was agreed that doors should be fixed to some cubicles.[11]

In the following year the Dolphin Club had club ladies wanting to swim, but the Baths Sub Committee had refused to allow men in the pool to teach them. It was decided in May that clubs should only use the Cleveland site on alternate Tuesdays for river swimming, not every Tuesday as before, but that they could play water polo in the Cleveland Pool on those nights.[12]

Councillors were faced with more formalised representations from the clubs in 1905. A joint letter from the YMCA and Dolphin clubs was read out to the Baths Committee. The clubs used facilities at the Cleveland Baths site for river bathing, but early morning and alternate Tuesdays as currently allocated was insufficient for this purpose. The clubs pointed out that they had left a bathing station by the bridge, in deference to public opinion, to use the Cleveland pool for a base, but they had not anticipated these restrictions to swimming times. The Sub Committee agreed to consider the position with swimming clubs and boat clubs, but in the meantime emphasised that proper costumes were to be worn – it is not recorded what the councillors' problem was with club members' bathing costumes.[13]

Joint working between the clubs continued. For a period until 1908, the YMCA and Dolphin clubs joined forces to create a Bath United squad to compete in swimming races and water polo competitions. Water polo is a highly physical and demanding sport – it had been part of the summer Olympics programme since 1900.

The introduction of national standards was seen in 1914 when the Bath Dolphin Summer Gala, held at the Cleveland Baths, was conducted using ASA (Amateur Swimming Association) rules. The Gala was as popular as ever, with spectators on the banks of

Photograph of the Cleveland Baths in circa 1910 including Samuel Inkerman Bailey. COURTESY OF HIS FAMILY DESCENDANTS

the river, livened by the music wafting over from the opposite bank where the Larkhall Flower Show was in full swing.[14]

The Baths' Improvements and Popularity

Athorough cleansing of the Baths encouraged swimmers to take an early dip in May 1908, the morning temperature of the water being 54 degrees centigrade. In the summer of that year, an extraordinary 45,000 visits were recorded at the Baths, and at times they were seriously overcrowded. Unemployed workers were drafted in by the council to create a pool extension that cost £700 and was unveiled in the summer of 1909. This eastern extension, which increased the length of the baths from 80 to 120 feet, was 30 feet wide and 4 feet deep. Extra dressing rooms were also provided. A few of the cubicles retained some interior joinery and fittings that are likely to have been installed in this Edwardian period.

The council's concern with unemployment was highlighted again when in 1909 it was proposed to spend a further £200 on improving the Baths. The Bath Chronicle and Weekly Gazette reported that: *'The work is desirable more especially as the larger proportion of the money will be spent in wages and the whole of the labour will be selected from the unemployed.'*[15] It was to be a few years before these works took place.

Between 1910 and 1914, the main bath was at last separated from the river, introducing mains water. The eastwards extension of the bath was added to increase capacity – that gave the main pool its P shape rather than the original D shape. Terraces and shelters were installed to the east of the existing changing rooms. The upper pool had an added rockery and shelters at either end. It was paved in the base and lined with brick. These were substantial improvements for a public facility in a period when public resources were constrained. They reflected popular public demand, which was well evidenced by numbers of people swimming.

Regulations issued by the council in relation to mixed bathing. COURTESY OF BATH RECORD OFFICE: ARCHIVES & LOCAL STUDIES

CITY OF BATH.

CLEVELAND BATHS.

REGULATIONS

WITH RESPECT TO

MIXED or FAMILY BATHING.

1. The bath must be cleared of general bathers at 1.30 p.m. on Thursdays.

2. Curtains must be placed in front of dressing boxes used by bathers while mixed or family bathing is in progress.

3. The dressing boxes and promenade on one side of the bath will be reserved exclusively for the use of women, and on the opposite side for men.

4. Bathers must enter and leave the water and use the promenade of the bath at that side only of the bath on which their dressing boxes are placed.

5. All dressing boxes must be kept closed whilst in use.

6. No bather shall leave or open his or her dressing box unless completely attired or in bathing costume.

7. All males must wear the recognised University bathing costume, and all females must wear an approved costume.

8. No bather will be admitted unless accompanied by a person of the opposite sex, except in the case of children accompanied by their parents or guardians.

9. A male and female attendant shall be on duty during the whole time mixed or family bathing is in progress.

10. The entrance fee for Adults shall be 6d. for each person, and for children under 15 years of age, accompanied by either their parents or guardians, 3d.

11. Spectators will be charged for admittance at the same rate as bathers.

FRED^K. D. WARDLE,
Town Clerk.

GUILDHALL, BATH,
3rd June, 1913.

PRINTER—J. GRANT MELLUISH, BROAD STREET, BATH.

In 1911 the 'phenomenal rush' to use the Baths was reported – no fewer than 88,884 baths were taken there in the summer and autumn.[16] These included state school swimming use, as the Bathwick schools competed for a cup. Most swimmers were male, as evidenced by the limited access for women: *'The fair sex have the use of the Baths from 9.30–10.30 on Sunday morning and an additional hour on Wednesday evenings.'*[17] It had been an exceptionally hot and fine high season, one of those notoriously good summers before the First World War.

A discussion at the same council meeting in 1911 showed that cost effectiveness was a continuing priority. There was a proposal that instead of full mains water supply, a natural water source should be used, to minimise the volume of mains water needed: *'It appears that there is a flow of water from the slopes above the Warminster Road which runs into a tank near Sydney House…it is proposed to take to the Baths a three-inch pipe for it is realised that it would form a valuable auxiliary to the present supply.'* There is no record of this cost-saving suggestion being implemented, and the Corporation made a further investment – to keep the water clean, a centrifugal pump was fixed, capable of pumping 20,000 gallons per hour.[18]

Mixed Bathing

Samuel Inkerman Bailey, as Superintendent, would have had to contend with the public reactions to mixed bathing at the Baths, which was 'inaugurated' – with some publicity – on 12th June 1913. Mixed bathing facilities at the Cleveland Baths were available during very specific timeframes. That is the context of a feature headed 'Arm Chair Musings', published in the local press six years later:[19]

'Amenities of bathing. Mixed bathing which is a weekly privilege at the Cleveland Bath, if indeed it is a privilege, is not viewed with quite so much complacency in other places as it is in Bath. The mixing of the sexes is permitted in Ealing and members of the Wesleyan Church are very concerned. In their view, mixed bathing leads to promiscuous meetings and encourages young people to make chance acquaintanceships, a detrimental practice. The author thinks the church people protest too much because it does not need swimming to bring about chance meetings.'

But despite such objections, mixed bathing had been introduced nationally from the early 1900s. It was regarded as progressive and recognised the advantages of families being able to swim together. Legal segregation of beaches ended in Britain in 1901. The Cleveland Baths was by no means delayed in introducing mixed bathing – there were lido settings in London where it was not allowed until decades later.

New Regulations

The Corporation reflected its concern to influence behaviour at the improved Baths by introducing new regulations. In 1915 swimming at the reopened Cleveland Baths was allowed for half an hour only, with 'no loitering, no offensive language', restrictions on entry to the site, respect for others' property and bathing apparel, a ban on jumping from the bank to swim in the river, etc – these regulations are known informally by the Cleveland Pools Trust as the 'Rules of the Pools': the penalty for breach of any of the twelve bye-laws was a £5 fine.

These are a selection of the actual bye-law clauses:[20]

A person resorting to the open bathing place shall not knowingly remain therein for a longer period than half an hour;

A person resorting to the open bathing place shall not, by any improper or disorderly conduct, disturb or interrupt any other person in the proper use of such bathing place, or any officer, servant or person appointed or employed by the Council in the proper execution of his duty;

A person resorting to the bathing place shall not at any time whilst using such bathing place, use any indecent or offensive language, or behave in an offensive or indecent manner.

A person resorting to the open bathing place shall not enter or quit such bathing place otherwise than through the door, gate, wicket, passage, or opening appointed by the Council as the authorised means of entrance to, or egress from, such bathing place.

Implementation of these regulations coincided with the impending outbreak of the First World War and Superintendent Bailey's consequent departure from Bath to rejoin his ship.

Death of Samuel Inkerman Bailey

Despite his being 52 years of age, Samuel Inkerman Bailey volunteered for service a day before the proclamation to recall the Royal Navy reserves and two days before the UK declared war on 4th August 1914. He appears to have had no remaining reserve obligation and would not have been recalled, so this was an entirely voluntary act. He was not required for duty until 1915. This delay is not surprising in view of his age and the fact that there were many reservists and younger volunteers to be processed. Samuel sadly died, not in active service, but of food poisoning in Portsmouth on 11th October 1915. According to his obituary,[21] his wife Joanna received a letter to say he was ill on Thursday, 7th October. On Sunday, 10th October, she received a further communication and travelled to see him, but he had died before she arrived. Samuel Inkerman Bailey was buried in Bathwick Cemetery. At that time, their five children were aged 13, 11, 10, 7 and 5 years. Alice moved to Railway Cottage on Hampton Row in 1922 or 1923, and remained at that address until she died aged 77. Some of the descendants of Samuel and Alice live in the Bath area today.

The question arose as to how to fill the vacancy for Superintendent of the Cleveland Baths[22] created by the death of Mr Bailey. It was recommended by the Public Bathing Place Sub Committee[23] that the post be advertised at one guinea (21 shillings) per week, but that Mrs Bailey be given due notice to leave the house at Hampton Row, the tied accommodation that was associated with the Superintendent post. The Corporation rented the house at £16 per year, Mr Bailey having paid half the rent and the Corporation covering the rates. A discussion was held as to whether the new Superintendent should have the same privileges. One speaker observed that the job was worth one guinea per week without the house…It was decided to advertise the post at 25 shillings a week, the post holder to live within a reasonable distance of the pool.

A temporary appointment had been made after Samuel Bailey left Bath for his continuing naval service. A Mr Bolwell was appointed as Acting Superintendent. He was probably Edwin Bolwell, born in 1855, of Powlett Road, Bathwick. The Superintendent appointment remained unresolved in the spring of 1916 when councillors made reference to a man who was employed at the Waterworks providing some temporary cover. The scale of conscription to military service would have made it difficult to recruit from a broad field of applicants, as a special tribunal in the city was preoccupied with whether exemption from service at the Front was justified to cover key jobs and roles. In other circumstances, applications may have come from Bath Dolphin Club members, but nearly 40 of them were serving abroad. In the event, it was understandably considered that employment should be given to one of the injured men returning from the Front.

Eventually, Edward Ricketts was appointed as Superintendent after he had begun recovery from serious wounds arising from his war service – he was a resident of Twerton, Bath, who had served with the Coldstream Guards in the machine gun corps. He took up residence at first, in the cottage at the Cleveland Baths. He married, had two daughters, and brought up his family at Powlett Rd. Sadly, at nearly 60 years of age, in 1936 he was found dead as a result of suicide, having suffered from depression, probably since his war service.[24]

The Emphasis on Lifesaving During the First World War

In 1916 the Cleveland Baths had been thoroughly cleaned and renovated in readiness for the summer, and would be opened from Monday 1st May from 6.00a.m. to 8.00p.m. Attendances at the Cleveland Baths[25] reflected a very significant increase in popularity and commitment from schools in the city in relation to boys' swimming – over 15,000 schoolboys used the Baths that year, compared to 8,000 in 1915. One of the most thriving swimming classes in Bath in 1917 was at St. Mark's School (Lyncombe), started by the Headmaster, Mr L. England, 'a firm believer in organised games and recreation':

'He believes teaching and practising the skill is the most important subject in the curriculum and one he put into action when he was appointed in 1912, at first at the Cleveland Baths and later at the Cross Baths. Mr Harris, a member of staff, was the first instructor and Mr Beamish later began lifesaving classes with gratifying results – in 1916 ten boys obtained the Royal Life Saving medal. In the girls' department Mr England observed that Miss Byard was doing similar good work since her appointment last year.'[26]

Miss Byard was Bertha Byard, aged 31 in 1916, the daughter of a Bath corn dealer; she was to remain single and to continue teaching in Bath for some decades.

A speaker at the prize giving at St. Mark's School in the previous year had commented that swimming classes had only just begun when he was a boy and that the classes had been at the Cleveland Baths, but that they were later held at the Cross Bath. Lifesaving was now part of the curriculum, and certificates were handed to a number of boys. The speaker said that watches had been handed to two boys from the school who had saved life from drowning.[27]

The swimmers' Life Saving Society had been founded in 1891. There was a recognition that speed swimming was of little use in lifesaving and that specific lifesaving techniques should be recognised. King Edward VII became patron of the Life Saving Society in 1904. Medals were awarded by the Royal Humane Society. By 1912 the techniques of immediate rescue from drowning, then bringing a rescued person ashore, followed by resuscitation methods, were promoted in detail. The increase in boys' swimming after 1915 and the concern with proficiency in lifesaving reflected First World War preoccupations, including the context of the war at sea. Unrestricted submarine warfare made all allied vessels in British coastal waters a target. For teenage boys anticipating conscription, swimming proficiency and lifesaving competence took on a new significance.

Modern photograph of the Pulteney Weir, Bath. The Weir was the starting point for races to the Bathampton Weir, in the early decades of the 20th century. ISTOCK.COM/ALEXKOZLOV

Young Women's Swimming in Bath

Interestingly, in relation to teaching swimming for girls at school, this advertisement appeared regularly in the local press throughout the year:

Duke Street Girls' School

1 and 2, Duke St, Bath
Principals: The Misses Cleghorn and Clements
Preparation for Examinations. Prospectuses on Application.
Hockey, Tennis, Gymnasium and Swimming.

Misses Cleghorn and Clements could take advantage of their school's proximity to the Avon, so that swimming at the Baths in suitable weather was possible by walking over the nearby Pulteney Bridge and then on to the Baths – a distance of one mile. Grace Cleghorn was born in London in 1880, where she taught before coming to Bath. Edith Clements was born in Canterbury in 1874, awarded her degree by the University of London in 1900 and was to retire in Bath, continuing to coach young women. As joint principals they had taken on their responsibilities while in their thirties after the retirement of the older female principals and teachers. The school employed swimming instructresses who were married women, and it was to participate in annual swimming competitions held at the Royal Baths in the spa complex, entering pupils for lengths, diving and lifesaving.

Women's and girls' swimming attracted positive media attention when several members of the Bath Lady Dolphin Swimming Club attempted, on Thursday, 14th August 1919, to swim from weir to weir (Pulteney Weir to Bathampton Weir), two of the members being fifteen and sixteen years old respectively. Another member, Miss V. Dabner, aged eighteen, planned to swim the double distance, a six-mile swim, and she started from Pulteney Bridge at about 2.00p.m., swimming breaststroke at a 'good speed'. The others started from Bathampton Weir when she arrived there at 4.00p.m. It was estimated they would be at Pulteney Bridge by about 5.30p.m. – this estimate was accurate.[28] Violet Dabner was born in Bath, the daughter of a brewer, living in Upper Weston. Her fellow swimmers included Hilda Cantelow, who was born in Bath in 1899 and was brought up by an uncle who was a plumber, living in a small cottage in Camden, Bath. The social backgrounds of dedicated female swimmers had become more diverse.

Appointing the Lady Attendant

A contentious discussion livened the Waterworks Committee in relation to the Lady Attendant's appointment at the Cleveland Baths:

'Mr Hallett chaired a meeting of the Public Bathing Places sub-committee. It was reported that Miss James being willing to take the duties of attendant on ladies' days at the wages paid last year, was appointed. Councillor Evans proposed an amendment that Miss Lovell be offered the post at 10s a week instead of the 15s she considered she was entitled to receive when she was first approached.

This was seconded and carried whereupon the chairman left the chair and resigned the chairmanship. Alderman Gould stated that the other candidate Miss Lovell asked for 150 per cent salary on pre-war prices. Both the ladies had been previously employed at the Baths...On enquiry the committee found that Miss Lovell wanted an increase on re-engagement but Miss James was willing to undertake it at the same rate as last year. He recommended the appointment of Miss James. He had always taken a great interest in the Cleveland Baths and was sorry to leave the subcommittee. He asked the committee not to confirm this amendment. Alderman Gould said Miss Lovell had enlisted the influence of someone on the committee [Mr Evans: NO].'

Councillor Evans asked for the right to reply to these statements. Miss Lovell was not a personal friend of his, nor was her father...The duties at the Baths occupied about 15 hours a week and Miss Lovell filled in her time as instructress at the Royal Baths. She was proficient in swimming... Eventually the sub committee's report was adopted.[29]

Kate Beatrice Lovell was born in Somerset in 1889. She was recorded in the 1911 Census as having private means. Miss James was most probably Nellie James, born in Bath in 1880, one of her sisters being involved in running the Bath Dolphin Club. Both sisters became teachers and remained unmarried.

More widely in England, improvement in provisions for serious female swimmers came slowly. Contemporary planners considered that the demands of family restricted women's needs and desire for access to facilities, and therefore they allocated women less in terms of pool size and time slots. By 1904, 57 out of London's 63 baths had limited facilities for women, including 10 which had 'women only' pools (Horwood, 2000, pp.656-57).

Early in this period, women's bathing dresses were still very substantial and impractical, often made of wool, using 8-9 yards of fabric. But the design of women's' bathing dresses became simpler with contrasting white stripe trimming. Soft ballerina-type slippers, with lacing up to the knee, were worn to protect feet on pebble beaches. Men's costumes were known as tank suits – they were still substantial, in dark solid colours, extending to the elbow and below the knee.

Competitive swimming was highlighting the need for more functional swimming costumes. By the 1912 Olympics when women first competed, competitive female wore a similar costume to the men – a one-piece, dark coloured thick cotton sleeveless garment to the mid – thigh, cut wide at the shoulders or with a cap sleeve, with a high neck.

The introduction of 'bath gowns' in this country in 1910 to cover girls over fourteen years old when entering and leaving the water was undoubtedly the result of the contemporary furore over the more streamlined costumes, reflected in the words of the saucy music-hall song *When Maud Put Her New Bathing Costume On*, published in 1916 (Horwood, 2000, pp.657-58).

Mixed bathing at a few local pools was introduced, facilitated by the allocation of separate changing rooms for women. Family bathing also began to be encouraged. Swimming clubs were more commonly established in areas with a larger population and would have taught more swimming strokes – the backstroke swimming stroke was first officially used at the Olympics in 1900 but it had been used in some competitive swimming decades earlier. The front crawl was introduced in the early 1900s.

Examples of Pools Constructed in the Early 1900s

An indication of the growing interest in public swimming can be seen in the increased number of pools that were built after 1900. There are some features in the history of these pools that resonate with the history of the Cleveland Baths in the same period – councils being motivated to provide public facilities, the introduction of the mains water supply, the use of the labour of unemployed men and municipal concerns relating to public health.

An interesting example of a pool being built in the early Edwardian period is Tooting Bec Lido, which originated as Tooting Bathing Lake, constructed during a few months in 1906. It was the initiative of Reverend John Hendry Anderson, Rector of Tooting, as a project to provide work for unemployed men – the employment opportunity was the motivation. The pool at Tooting was designed partly as a communal bath to recognise needs arising from the lack of domestic facilities. An earth ramp was constructed to conceal the bathers from the nearby common. Mixed bathing was not introduced there until 1931.

The original King's Meadow municipal pool on the Thames at Reading first opened to the public in 1902. It was river-fed, built to allow women to bathe privately. Mains water supply was not introduced until the 1950s.

An indoor municipal pool example is the striking Moseley Road Baths in Birmingham. Opened in 1907, they included private baths (the original time limit was 30 minutes) and offered two pools. In addition to the original glazed brickwork and leaded windows with tinted glass, the steam-heated drying racks still survive.

Bramley Baths in Leeds, originally an iron foundry, opened as a pool and bath house in 1904, so that local people could wash, swim and enjoy the fashionable Russian steam baths.

The examples given above were in areas of substantial urban population. The question of the extent of public subsidy was a very different consideration for a sizeable city council. In the small city of Bath, that debate was a more problematic balance. The Public Bathing Place Sub Committee agreed that there should be charges for swimming in 1921, although this was not a universal view. The adult charge would be 3d and season tickets 7s 6d, under sixteens would be charged 1d and their season tickets cost 5s, but the children's bath was to remain free. Councillors took into account that in 1920, the Baths had been a cost of £270 to ratepayers.[30]

Positive considerations were the continuing use of the Cleveland Baths by established clubs and the growing public interest in diving displays. Local residents who had sufficient income were willing to pay for the thrill of experiencing feats of diving – not simply spectacular display, but also demonstrations of skill by men and women who otherwise may have taken part in competitions in this country or internationally. That public interest in athleticism and proficiency is explored in the next chapter.

Chapter 7

Display, Diving and Feats – the 1920s and 1930s

'It is desirable that every town possessing natural swimming privileges or capacious baths, should have its own tournaments and rewards for excellence in swimming.'[1]

The popularity of competitive swimming and display diving that could be seen nationally in the 1920s was also reflected in Bath and will be discussed in this chapter. The influential growth of the lido movement is also outlined, along with issues for the Bath Corporation in relation to the Cleveland Baths, in a period when public service budgets were under very significant pressure.

Swimming Displays in Bath

Feats of diving were very popular with the Bath crowds in the early 1920s. The development of technical diving skills with competent and sustained training meant that proficient divers could amaze poolside audiences – without resorting to the stunts as practised by Captain Evans. It was important for the Baths to be able to stage some displays featuring 'star' swimmers or divers and regular competitions, for the reason that such events were very popular in this period. These events were income-generating activities to supplement individual swimming entry costs and club fees. The total of annual entry payments of individuals could fluctuate, depending on the weather during the summer season.

At this point in the early 1920s, the Beamish Stage on the Avon, which was closer to the city centre, in the area of the current Bath rugby ground, was a serious competitor with the Baths for events and galas. Though some performers swam at both sites, notably Irene Snelgrove and the Olympic swimmer Paul Radmilovic. The Beamish Stage was a diving platform built to international standards – this structure and the Beamish Cup were named to acknowledge the contribution of George Peete Beamish, Inspector of the Bath Police and Town Clerk. He was exceptional in his active promotion of swimming and lifesaving, and served Bath for 20 years, before his death aged 45, in November 1920. In relation to displays, the diving board at the Baths was not of an international standard, though the Baths could cater for fun displays, water polo matches and, of course, swimming for all ages.

An event arranged by the Boy Scouts Life Savers at the Beamish Stage, competing for the Beamish Cup, was staged to involve three Boy Scout teams in swimming and lifesaving competitions. This type of event could have been held at the Cleveland Baths, resulting in a loss of potential income – a difficulty for the Baths when it was important to maintain such income. Fortunately, in 1925 the Cup competition returned to be held at the Baths.[2]

In July 1920 there was an event at the Beamish Stage and a similar event at the Baths, with competitions and stunts performed by Radmilovic. He caused much laughter at the Baths with his imitations of a porpoise swimming and of a monkey on a stick. His swimming prowess and extraordinary agility was illustrated in backward swimming, somersaults, 'seal' swimming and diving, and his 'waltzing swim'. Irene Snelgrove was most often seen at the Baths taking part in water polo matches, as she was a regular team member with the Bath Dolphins.

Two days later, Irene Snelgrove was performing on the Beamish site. Her display consisted of a standing dive from the board, backward somersault dive, running dive and high dives. Irene originated from Weston-super-Mare and was a student at the catering college in Bath. She was born in Swindon in 1897, but spent most of her life at Weston-super-Mare, where her income as a performance swimmer enabled her to spend her later years living at Crosby Hall, on the beachfront.[3]

In that same summer in 1920, Radmilovic took part in competitive water polo in the Cleveland Baths – he was to win a Gold Medal in the Olympics held in Antwerp a few weeks later. Paolo Francesco Radmilovic, nicknamed 'Raddy', was born in 1886, the son of Croatian/Irish parents from Cardiff. He was an outstanding water polo player and competitive swimmer who represented Great Britain at four Summer Olympics, winning four Gold Medals across three successive Olympic Games, the last being achieved at the 1920 Summer Olympics in Antwerp – the water polo team competitions were held in late August. The medals must have been viewed with keen interest and celebration in Bath, given that Radmilovic had played water polo at the Cleveland Baths during the previous month.

'Raddy' was appointed as a Dolphin Club Vice President in 1922. He was to take over the running of the York House hotel in Bath, and the Angel Inn in Westgate St, relinquishing these interests early in the Second World War. Later in life, he ran the Imperial Hotel in Weston-super-Mare – a blue plaque was installed there in 2017 to honour his achievements.

Balancing the Books – the Corporation's Subsidy

There were continuing tensions for Bath Corporation councillors throughout the 1920s in relation to the level of income from the Cleveland Baths. In many years the income received did not reach the optimum level that was required. The impact for the Corporation of the relatively low-income level in the early 1920s was that several hundred pounds in subsidy had to be provided from the rates. The Waterworks Committee was required by the Corporation to balance its books and not to continue to incur a deficit. Since the 1890s, the commitment of a number of Corporation councillors to public provision in Bath had been apparent in the representations they made to their colleagues. One of these was

Alderman Gould, who resigned from the Waterworks Committee in 1920 over differences in policy and priority – he had been a significant advocate of the benefits of the Cleveland Baths. One of the improvements to the Baths that had been proposed and shelved was the installation of a water chute. A noticeable number of boys were seen swimming in the river, no doubt because they could not afford the charge to enter the Baths in a period of economic depression – councillors were seriously worried about the effects of the poor water quality in the river, but acknowledged that they could not stop boys swimming there.

The growth in Dolphin Club membership led to expectations about increased income for the council. There was debate at the Bath Corporation Waterworks Committee after the close of the summer season in 1921 about the discount given to the Dolphin Club for use of the Cleveland Baths and the Committee's disappointment with the income from the Club:

'...the results from the first year of charging for the use of the pool (3d for adults and 7s 6d for season tickets, 6s as a concession to the Dolphin Club). The club had let the committee down because it bought only 3 tickets. They preferred to swim in hot water and pay 7d a time for that. It had been hoped that charging would increase revenue but that had taken only £66 4s 6d. There had been some outgoings but it was thought worth continuing the policy another year…It was decided to continue charges as before but not to give discount to clubs.'[4]

The Corporation's consideration of club swimming was understandably different from the problematic debates about subsidising the summer season for individual swimmers. Local clubs could forecast regular use by predictable numbers of committed swimmers who paid membership fees that gave clubs a regular income. They could exert influence as an effective lobby and take advantage of the developing national profile of swimming clubs.

The sensitivity of the level of charges and attention to monitoring their impact was demonstrated again in April 1923 when reduced charges were proposed – the adult swimming charge was reduced from 3d to 2d, but at the same time it was agreed that the Bath Dolphin Club should be charged 10s for the year, for the use of the dressing shed. Again, the implication was that a club was more able to afford those costs, and the Corporation wished to maximise attendance by individuals.[5] In that same year, the new indoor baths in Beau St were opened – they were to have long-term use by the Dolphin Club.

Bath, the most historic of the spa towns, aimed to continue its spa treatment, despite the prevailing difficulties, especially between the wars. In 1927 the Royal Bath was redesigned inside in neo-Georgian style by the Corporation Spa Committee, which reported, however, that in 1928–32 its total receipts fell by 10 per cent (Hembry, 1997, p.226).

In January 1928, the issue of the financial subsidy of the Cleveland Baths had re-emerged. Alderman C.H. Long, who acknowledged that he had not visited the open-air Baths for over 40 years, raised a concern as to whether the previous year's expenditure of £234 on the Baths was justified, in the face of the income of only £30.[6] The justification presented to the Waterworks Committee was that 1,640 men, 5,497 boys, 743 women and 1,320 people on mixed bathing days had used the Baths in the previous year. The annual Scout swimming and diving event held at the Cleveland Baths in July 1928 demonstrated the participation of schools – notably Kingswood School, Manvers St and Oldfield Schools.

Eighteen months later, in 1929, there were rumours about the closure of the Baths, though in that year the council took action to chlorinate the pools in order to alleviate concerns about health risks highlighted by the Medical Officer of Health.[7] The health concerns may have been partly linked to the 1928 typhoid outbreak in Bathwick Hill that was traced to springs polluted by sewage.

The popularity of swimming, combined with social welfare considerations especially applying to the more disadvantaged areas in Bath, influenced councillors' debates and decision making. From time to time, some councillors acknowledged the need to build swimming baths in Twerton, to the south of the city centre, recognising population levels and relative social disadvantage, but that initiative was not taken forward, probably due to affordability. Other councillors advocated that baths should be built at Newbridge or Oldfield Park – these representations reflected the demand for accessible swimming provision in areas of the city with substantial residential populations on average or low incomes.

The wider economic context of recession and social need generated more pressing demands and financial constraint. While conditions in Bath did not compare to the far worse conditions in larger urban areas, some 10 per cent of men in the city were recorded as out of work in the Census of 1931. Housing conditions in parts of the city were overcrowded and insanitary, probably contributing to a spike in tuberculosis cases in the early 1930s. But by 1931 the council had completed new housing provision in Odd Down, Larkhall and Southdown (Davis and Bonsall, 2006, pp.259–264).

An interesting argument was put forward with regard to the need for a properly constructed bathing place with dressing accommodation, at Batheaston, to the east of the city. The idea was put forward in 1933 by the Misses Tollemache of Batheaston Villa, who had been active suffragettes and advocates of progressive social change:

'It seems better that a public body representing the people should have the management of such a scheme…our scheme would employ men on work for public benefit, not merely to make our own homes more comfortable; for surely everyone wants their children to learn to swim, even if they do not wish to swim themselves?'[8]

In the event, the parish council decided that such a scheme could not be considered in the current circumstances. The argument concerning social responsibility, of public benefit including male employment, resonated with Bath Corporation's debates in 1900 and 1901 that had led to the improvements to the Cleveland Baths.

Through the 1920s and 1930s, Bath Corporation councillors would be aware that clubs, display diving and competitions were key to boosting income levels and promoting community engagement as participants or as spectators in the enjoyment of skilled swimming. The Bath Dolphin Swimming Club organised its indoor swimming at the new baths known as the New Royal Baths, but it continued a long association with the Cleveland

Baths for outdoor swimming and as a venue for the annual galas that attracted supportive crowds. The First World War had inevitably brought about the limiting of the Dolphin Club's activities, but a few months after the end of the war the club benefited from a surge of new members. A noteworthy trend was the continuing growth of the Club Women's Section, with 72 new members joining in 1919.[9]

The Club's regular use of the Cleveland Baths for outdoor use continued. In the high season of 1925, the Bath Dolphin 'hut' at the Cleveland Baths was full, while quite a number of the Club members were at the Baths for their daily dip before breakfast.[10] In that year, Mr Ricketts was reappointed as Superintendent at the Baths and Miss James was reappointed as Ladies' Superintendent.[11] Mr Ricketts was Edward Walter Ricketts, a First World War Coldstream Guards veteran. Miss James was very likely to have been Nellie Maud James, born in Bath in 1880. She had swum at Bath Dolphin club races in 1921 and one of her sisters was a Dolphin treasurer.

Development of Clubs, Women's Swimming and Costumes

By the early decades of the 20th century, swimming interests in this country were being influenced by the formation of local clubs like the Bath Dolphin Club, which were often affiliated with the Amateur Swimming Associations for each of the countries of the UK. An associated key development was that swimming had developed into a range of disciplines that encompassed: recreational swimming; competitive sports of swimming, diving, synchronised swimming and water polo; and the humanitarian field of aquatic lifesaving.[12] The butterfly swimming stroke developed in this period, combined with breaststroke leg kick. Swimming schools were established in larger population centres, and there were numerous swimming manuals on the market.

As we know from the history of the Cleveland Baths, prior to 1918 swimming competitions were held in any sized body of water that was available, but in the first decades of the 20th century, standardised pool sizes were introduced, and the municipal sector was the predominant provider of swimming pools to the public.[13]

By the end of the 1930s, few women-only clubs were still in existence – most clubs were for both genders but had separate competitive events for men and women.[14] Women's swimming was given a further boost when the first women swam the Channel in 1926 and 1928. Members of women's clubs, and women swimmers generally, were starstruck by the feats of individual swimmers such as Agnes Beckwith, who swam five miles in the Thames, from London Bridge to Greenwich (Landreth, 2017, pp.84–86).

Nationally, there were more communal areas at pools and fewer restricted internal spaces, and communal changing and showering facilities began to be provided. However, where swimming baths were used by both sexes at different hours, it was often the case that women and girls were allocated a smaller proportion of time, with little or no opportunity for bathing on Saturdays or holidays (Campbell, 1918, p.63).

Restrictive bye-laws were still in place in many areas with regard to mixed bathing in rivers, lakes and pools, whereas in the early decades of the 20th century there were relatively few restrictions on sea bathing. Margaret Nevinson, a British suffrage campaigner, observed:

'Few realise the hard work that their mothers and grandmothers have had to get the taboo removed from fresh-water swimming for women. I remember how bitter it was in our childhood to be told, when we saw our brothers going joyously out to swim in any river or pond handy: 'Little ladies may only bathe in the sea; God made the canals and rivers for boys. You are very rude girls to want to go.' (Landreth, 2017, pp.140-41).

Swimming costumes for both men and women had become streamlined and more functional, suitable for competitive swimming. The US company Jantzen had developed a finer-knit rib-stitch wool fabric, and advertised 'swimming costumes' as opposed to 'bathing costumes'. Fabrics used were still not ideal, as quick-drying artificial stretch fabrics such as Lycra were not produced until a few decades later.

Both men and women wore sleeveless singlet -style costumes later in the period. In the UK a mass-produced Speed Suit for men was popular. It incorporated fitted trunks. Women's costumes might have a skirt though both skirt and shorts had to be a specific length above the knee. In 1928 the 'racerback' swimsuit for women was introduced by Speedo, optimised to fit body shape and allowing for much greater arm movement. Rayon was introduced for these sleeker swimsuits but it was not sufficiently durable. Shirred elastic cotton was more common. This era saw the decline of the wool swimsuit for both men and women.

The 1930s saw women's costumes having more exposed shoulders and lower necks, sometimes with a plunging back. Leg lines were cut higher to the upper thigh. In the early 1930s it was not considered respectable for men to be bare chested, but later in this period shorts and swimming trunks were introduced for men's swimming. These might incorporate a fly front and buckled belt to make them resemble more acceptable daywear. In 1935, male competitors were bare chested for the first time in an international competition.

Social and Cultural Influences – the Origins of the Lido Movement

The physical health of the nation was a growing concern after the First World War. It had been found that some 40 per cent of potential troops who had been given medical examinations were unfit for service abroad in terms of height and strength (Ayriss, 2011). Food deficiencies and shortages during the war led to an increase in the incidence of rickets and tuberculosis. These factors, combined with the trend of greater leisure time, led to a more pronounced interest in the benefits of outdoor pools.

Physical culture in this period was characterised by a belief that exercising, whilst in itself good for the body, was enhanced through exposure to sunlight. This emphasis led to a boom in outdoor physical activity – rambling, cycling and open-air swimming amongst others (Marino, 2010, pp.39-40). Lidos built in England in the 1920s reflected the concern to provide substantial space alongside pools, for other forms of exercise. Jesus Green Swimming Pool in Cambridge, completed in 1923, is an existing example of that type of functional design.

The 1930s saw a rapid increase in lidos in the UK, with over 160 being built in that decade. They were associated with the cultural promotion of exercise, including swimming, in the open air and sunshine. These lidos had characteristic decorative Art Deco-style features. Saltdean Lido is an outstanding illustration of Art Deco with its striking modernist 'cruise ship' design completed in 1938. A few years earlier, Plymouth's Tinside Lido had been opened in 1935, a strikingly curved saltwater pool overlooking the sea, again with immediately

Modern photograph of Saltdean Lido, built in 1938, showing its Art Deco design. iStock.com/ Nickos

recognisable Art Deco style. In that same year, Penzance's Jubilee Pool, built into the Battery Rocks, was opened, marketing its Cubist design for the diving platform and steps.

Traditional design influences more redolent of existing parks' and gardens' architecture were apparent when the Sandford Parks Lido in Cheltenham opened in 1936, at the initiative of the local authority. The sizeable main pool – a standardised 165 feet by 90 feet, as advocated by the Amateur Swimming Association, was complemented by a children's pool and café. A cascade aeration water feature was quite a sensation (Barton, 2007).

The largest pool in Europe, the Tropicana at Weston-super-Mare, opened in 1937 and featured tiered diving structures, a beach-like aspect with shallow water and sizeable spectator stands. A later lido was Portishead, originally planned in the 1920s, then shelved for more than three decades, and after a few years' technical setbacks, finally opening in 1962 (Birkinshaw, 2018).

The lido (from the Latin litus, meaning 'shore') characteristically provided open-air swimming with space for sunbathing and exercise; swimming competitions were held regularly and most lidos provided ample room for spectators (Ayriss, 2012, p.98).

So, how did the Cleveland Baths relate to the lido movement? Although the Baths were more than a century older than the pools constructed in the context of the 1920s' and 1930s' lido movement, this national wave of enthusiasm for outdoor swimming further changed the perception of the Baths in that period. The assumed health benefits of sun exposure, the glamourisation of swimming and the novelty of free time would have brought the Cleveland Baths an additional level of popularity.

Councillors in the city recognised this by approving Art Deco-style features for the Baths, such as the 'fountain'. Paintwork was freshened – the Dolphin Club 1935 accounts show that it contributed to the costs. Yet the main pool buildings were Georgian in style, with additions on the site built in the Victorian era. At a time when futuristic images and cultural influences were in vogue, and the history of the Cleveland Baths was not widely disseminated, Bath's 'lido' would have appeared to be quirky and very old fashioned – yet the overriding consideration would have been the opportunity for open-air swimming at a reasonable cost for everyone.

In summary, the 1920s and 1930s saw radical changes in swimming culture in the UK that impacted on the Cleveland Baths. These changes ranged from the design of baths in the context of the lido movement, to the rapid growth of clubs, development of international standards in swimming and the phenomenon of swimming 'stars' who drew in large, excited crowds. This all contributed to increasing public engagement and personal interest in swimming as a desirable leisure activity.

The next chapter explores the functioning of the Baths in the Second World War and the years that followed – a challenging and disruptive period for the Cleveland Baths.

Poster showing female diver. COURTESY OF CATHERINE PHELPS WWW.CATHERINEPHELPS. COM

Chapter 8

'Bath's Own Little Lido' – the Second World War Years and Beyond

'British serving officers and men, and Polish airmen, have also been among those enjoying themselves in what has been called 'Bath's own little Lido.'[1]

This chapter assesses the impact of the Second World War on the Cleveland Baths, including the issues for the local council in this challenging period. The chapter goes on to examine the immediate post-war period, concluding with examples of impacts for other pools. The popularity of the Baths for local families was reflected in increasing use through the 1950s. The long-distance swimmer Commander Gerry Forsberg is profiled because he trained at the Cleveland Baths. Superintendent Lofty Harris and lifeguard Rowland Norris are also profiled.

The Baths in Wartime – Baptisms and Bombs

In 1941 over 8,000 bathers attended the Cleveland Baths for swimming, the highest number visiting in one week being over 1,800. The war had not appeared to have an adverse impact on attendance at this point, as it was reported that bathers' numbers were comparable with the pre-war years.[2] The Baths were open through the Whitsun holiday and were helpfully promoted as a 'Stay at Home' holiday activity in wartime conditions when travel arrangements were severely curtailed.

Derek Stone[3] remembered cycling to the Baths in the same period with friends from the Oldfield Park area. Derek taught himself how to swim in the Upper Pool, as no tuition was then available. His friend Russell Bell,[4] who sadly passed away in 2019, came to live in Bath in 1938, and he was one of the thousands of bathers using the Baths as a boy in 1941. Russell recalled that the Baths were open from April to October. Both men remembered that adult males wore an 'all in one' bathing costume, combining trunks with a vest in a single garment. In the early 1940s adult males often wore such a bathing costume, made from a dark woollen fabric.

Miss Jessie March was the Baths Supervisor in summer 1941:

'Bathers have handed in their cigarettes, marriage and death certificates, and ration books for me to look after. One actually gave me an orange – with instructions to guard it carefully!'[5]

Miss March's role no doubt complemented the work of a new appointee to the council – Mrs Raward, who was a swimming instructress appointed by the Bath Education Authority. Barbara Raward was born in Bristol in 1915, and held this role between her marriage in 1939 and the birth of her first child. She taught a large number of girls and boys to swim, including pupils at Weymouth House School, who held their swimming gala in July 1940. The characteristic wartime preoccupation with swimming skills and military service was reflected at the gala, where it was hoped that pupils would be joining the Royal Navy.[7] A positive development outside of existing club and schools' organised swimming was a joint effort by boys' clubs in Weston, the Abbey area and the relatively disadvantaged Milk St housing to join together, forming a single swimming club with the emphasis on learning how to swim.[8]

An unusual special event that was not open to the public took place in June 1941 when Jehovah's Witnesses used the Baths for a mass baptism. Some 46 complete immersion baptisms took place with an accompanying service – all of the candidates wore bathing dress. Those taking part in the baptism came from Gloucester, Wiltshire and Somerset, and even further afield.[9] This is the only record of such a ceremony being held at the Baths – their location not far from Bath Spa station could have been an advantage.

In the following year, enemy action damaged the Baths in April 1942 during the Bath Blitz, which was part of the Baedeker Raids – bombing raids with selected targets that had a social or cultural significance rather than say, dockland or the industrial areas that were extensively affected in Bristol. Three bombing raids in Bath took place over the weekend of 25–27 April 1942.[10] Over 400 people were killed, with more than 1,000 seriously injured, and more than 18,000 buildings were affected. Large numbers of Bathonians were displaced from their homes. The bomb damage to the Baths could have been linked to bombs being aimed at the station and trucks on the railway sidings.

The Baths then had to be repaired, resulting in a shorter season, with reopening in July that year – they were open from 9.00a.m. to 8.00p.m. during the summer season, again being promoted as a 'Stay At Home' leisure option.

Meanwhile, earlier in that month, attention was drawn to sewage pollution in the river between the Bathampton and Town Weirs[11], and there was a plea that the Cleveland Baths be reopened for public health reasons. Possibly in response to this public demand, the Baths were opened for the summer on 1st May 1943. There was a lowering of attendance rates, with an average of 100 per week through the season. The reduced numbers of swimmers could have been due to the numbers of adults involved in military service or associated deployment. Another factor could have been concern about the risk demonstrated by the bomb damage. Takings in September were ten shillings, the same amount as taken in the previous September – not enough, from the perspective of some councillors. In July that year, the prospect of closing the Baths had been discussed by councillors and rejected. Meanwhile, indoor swimming at the Beau St Baths during the war had been very popular.

A number of councillors were, however, focussed on the benefits of opening potential swimming baths for schools in Twerton, Oldfield Park and Odd Down, to benefit families on lower incomes, despite the economic uncertainty of the war years.

The viability of the Cleveland Baths was again called into question in December 1945 when the Waterworks Committee discussed a report on the summer season, a challenging season as there had only been one fine weekend. Though on that warm weekend, on 7th-8th July, some 600 swimmers had used the Baths. Over 5,000 adults and children had swum during the season, and the Boy Scouts' diving and lifesaving competitions had attracted enthusiastic audiences. September takings were low for the third year running. They were adversely affected by a terrific thunderstorm that swept ash and mud from the banks bordering the pool paths into the water, causing it to appear black.[12] The overall issue of concern for the council in 1945 was that there was a net deficit of over £300 linked to the budget for the Baths, which had to be met from the rates.

Other Pools and Lidos

The Second World War had a substantial impact on lidos: several were open for just a few seasons; most closed to the public for the duration. Some lidos in urban areas were put at the disposal of the National Fire Service. Sandford Park Lido in Cheltenham remained open during the war but adapted to wartime circumstances by letting wounded and recuperating soldiers use the pool. A retired sergeant described the Sandford Park pool as 'Heaven after Hell'. The Lido's records show that an average of 90,000 people used it between 1943 and 1945 (Birkinshaw, 2007).

Some lidos were damaged by bombing and failed to reopen for several years after the war due to shortages of materials for repair. Saltdean Lido did not reopen until 1964.

The well-known Greenbank Pool at Street drew in bathers from Wells and other Somerset towns – over 90,000 used the Pool in the summer season of 1959.[13] The Pool had been constructed by Bancroft Clark in 1937, complying with the wishes of his aunt Alice Clark in her will. The family had a philanthropic perspective in relation to the employment of local people at the Clarks' shoe factory. Alice Clark had a particular interest in providing bathing facilities for women and children, given the negative social attitudes to the habits of men who tended to bathe naked in the river Brue.[14]

The Post-War Baths: Harris, Norris and School Swimming for All

A dilemma arose in the summer of 1946 when there were no applications for the role of Cleveland Baths Caretaker:

'The post is open to either sex at a weekly wage of £4 to £5 and applicants must be good swimmers and qualified in life saving. It sounds like a job for an ex-Serviceman. The Waterworks Department will be glad of any applications.'[15]

The ex-serviceman who became Superintendent at the Baths in the late 1940s and early

1950s was Lofty Harris. Regrettably, little is known about him. His nickname derived from his height – a photograph shows him to be well over six feet tall, possibly six feet six inches, and he was renowned for keeping order with 'just a look'. Lofty was reputed to have been made homeless due to bomb damage in London after he was demobbed from his war service. He was said to live in 'squatted' ex-US airbase huts on Charmy Down, a local disused airfield. Lofty was also remembered for cycling every day to the Baths on his Claud Butler racing bike.

Lofty Harris would have been supported by Rowland Norris, who served as a volunteer lifeguard. Rowland discovered the Baths at the end of the war when he was twelve years old. As a boy he loved everything to do with water and boats. He first practised his skills as a lifeguard at the Beau St Baths, before his long-serving role at the Cleveland Baths in the 1950s and 1960s. He patrolled the pools perimeter and pulled anyone in danger, usually children, out of the water. He recalls that in the summer the Baths would be packed out with hundreds of bathers and that a lot of people brought picnics.[16] Rowland was a volunteer, so he was allowed to use the pool for free when he was off duty and the pool was empty. He was a strong swimmer and once, for a £10 bet, swam without pausing from Bathampton weir to Twerton weir. In the 1990s Rowland built a swimming pool in his garden for his daughter – she brought along her friends and other local children, with the result that word got around and inevitably there were queues to use his garden pool.

A young swimmer aged ten who started to swim at the Baths in 1948 was Dennis Toogood. Dennis went on to become a champion swimmer with the Bath Dolphins, then later to have honorary roles in the Amateur Swimming Association, becoming President of the Association in 2001.

In 1946 councillors again focussed on schools' swimming facilities in a context where it was understood that all school pupils should benefit from swimming. These discussions represented the shift over the previous decades from the Waterworks Committee deciding policy in regard to publicly owned swimming baths to the Education Committee advocating and deciding policy in relation to children's swimming. Public education with accompanying facilities was a firmly established priority with the city council at the time of the 1940s' national agenda, which included education reform as a key part of the creation of the welfare state.

The 1947 season at the Baths opened in June, after repairs to frost and flood damage, with a subsequent remarkably revived total attendance of 17,000 swimmers through the season. The City Treasurer's report in 1951[17] showed that attendance in 1947 was five times that in 1950. By 1949 the Waterworks Committee was facing an accumulated deficit of over £8,000 – but only a relatively small proportion of that was due to the Cleveland Baths, as there had been substantial war damage to the city water mains. Although prioritisation was necessary between allocation of resources to Sydney Gardens and the Baths, the Cleveland Baths had first call, reflecting the level of use, and the water supply was maintained.[18]

The following year saw some revived interest in club use of the Baths, with the city Waterworks Committee encouraging water polo.[19] The press advertisement for the opening of the Baths in May pronounced it to be the only open-air pool in the city.[20]

Commander Gerry Forsberg – a Notable Long-Distance Swimmer

In the mid-1950s, a young swimming enthusiast, John Dagger, who was twenty years later to become the Cleveland Bath's supervisor, had to rise early each morning for a few weeks to open the gate at the baths. His task was to admit a very dedicated long-distance swimmer for training in the main pool.

That long-distance swimmer was Commander Charles Gerald Forsberg. He was training to swim the English Channel, swimming length after length in the very cold water of the Baths in order to increase his stamina and acclimatise himself to very cold water temperatures. Norma Heath ran the kiosk in that period and she is said to have recalled that the Commander could swim the equivalent of six miles in the main pool without pausing.

Commander Forsberg, known as Gerry, was born in Vancouver in 1912. He began long-distance swimming in 1949, crossing the Solent and Morecambe Bay many times; there is a memorial to him on Morecambe Promenade. He was one of the greatest single influences in promoting long-distance swimming. His 40-year naval service, including involvement in the rescue of 500 people from the sea in wartime conditions, was honoured with an OBE in 1955.

Gerry became the thirteenth person to cross the English Channel – and did it in record time in 1957, taking just thirteen hours, thirteen minutes, from Dover to Cap Gris Nez in France. By 1982 Gerald Forsberg's swimming distances totalled over 8,800 miles and he had competed in over 211 open-water championships. He was still swimming in open-water events until two years before his death in 2000.

More widely, the 1950s saw a surge of interest in Channel swimming, with teams from many countries taking part in races, especially teams from Egypt. The sponsoring of Channel races by Butlins reflected the success of holiday camps created in the 1950s and 1960s, where swimming for fun and exercise was a significant feature. The closest Butlins camp to Bath was Minehead, which opened in 1962.

Perceptions of the Baths – Their Profile in the City

Interestingly, a press feature in the summer of 1950 commented on how a number of city features that were potentially of interest to visitors were 'hidden away' and not signposted:

'If you go to the average seaside resort…there are direction signs to the bathing beaches, the boating stations, the band concerts, the principal gardens and so on. At Bath, visitors are left to find most of these things out for themselves.

The open-air swimming bath, the river bathing and boating station are difficult for any stranger to find. Until one is near to them there is an almost complete absence of direction signs. Why? Surely, they are a valuable asset to the city now that summer is here?'[21]

The answers to these questions in relation to the Cleveland Baths are speculative – one distinct possibility is that the municipal focus for the Baths was on use by local residents in the city, rather than use by visiting tourists. Another lesser possibility is that, in a city with very significant historic features, such signage was not favoured for aesthetic reasons. There is no indication in the above feature that the Baths should be signposted because they represented an aspect of the city's Georgian heritage.

Seven years later, another press comment demonstrates that the history of the Baths was neither understood nor recognised:

'Yes, the Cleveland Baths, those funny little whitewashed baths hiding, as if in shame, tucked behind the trees, a dog's paddle from the river at Bathwick. Strange that anyone should have built swimming baths out there. Who did build them anyway? Must be pretty old. The truly strange thing is that no one really seems to know now, when and why, the Cleveland Baths came about.'[22]

It was to be several decades later that sustained research into the history of the Cleveland Baths generated knowledge and understanding of the Baths' age and origins. Meanwhile, an approach to social history focussing on contact with previous pool users generates insights into the use of the Baths and, importantly, gives detail of the experience of local swimmers. We are fortunate to be able to draw on the memories of people who enjoyed the Baths in their youth. The next chapter includes extracts from interviews with a number of those individuals.

Aerial view showing the Kennet & Avon Canal and Kensington Meadows on the opposite bank of the Avon.
COURTESY OF THE
CLEVELAND POOLS TRUST

Chapter 9

Swimmers' Memories of the 1950s and 1960s at the Baths

This chapter has the benefit of drawing richly on the memories of some of those who swam as children in the Baths in the 1950s and 1960s. Observations on relevant aspects of social history and issues for the City Council are also included.

Swimmers Recall Their Youth at the Baths

The relatively cheap fun and exercise at the pools was highlighted by Jean Russell (née Hooper), who reflected that she spent much of her free time in the summer in the late 1940s and early 1950s swimming at the Cleveland Baths:[1] *'It cost 4d to get in which was a lot of money to a child then, but there wasn't much else to spend your money on – the "2 and 9s" at the cinema was too pricey!'*

Jean Russell, who attended Oldfield Girls School, often went alone to Cleveland Baths because there was always someone there who she knew. Pupils at Walcot Girls School could swim before Jean could, which frustrated her. She learned to swim in the shallow end of the main pool but it wasn't until she was thirteen years old that she 'got her big toe off the bottom of the pool'. Once she got the hang of

Bathers in the 1960s. Photograph from the Wessex Water archive.
COURTESY OF THE MUSEUM OF BATH AT WORK

swimming, she immediately swam eighteen lengths until she was so exhausted and cold that she came out with blue lips and felt quite unwell, but, like other first-time distance swimmers, she was very proud of herself.

Jean went on to swim for her school and came third in the Schoolgirls Championship of Bath. She remembers that when arriving at the Baths in those days, *'you had to come through the archway, and your first task was to look on the slate to check the temperature of the water. It was*

Young bather on the pool steps in the 1960s. Photograph from the Wessex Water archive. COURTESY OF THE MUSEUM OF BATH AT WORK AND MATTHEW CROFT

tempting to go back home if it wasn't warm enough!' A very tall Superintendent would greet her (he would have been Lofty Harris).

Jean would choose a cubicle to change in and leave her clothes on the bench inside. Girls often had to share a cubicle, '*but there were no phones and jewellery to worry about back then…Some swimmers changed behind canvas at the shallow end of the pool but it felt more private in the cubicles, where you thought your clothes were safer and less likely to get wet.*'

Jean recollects that: '*You took the right money for swimming only because there was nothing else to buy, no shop or café. Everyone took their own drinks and sandwiches because you were allowed to stay all day.*' The 'right money' that Jean remembered to take for the entrance fee in summer 1957 would have been 4d for children and 6d for adults, the Baths being open from 2.00p.m. to 8.00p.m. In today's money values, that adult cost would be approximately £1.50, so the Baths were widely accessible to most families with different income levels in the city, unless they wanted to swim every day, as some young people did.

Ivor Gibbs remembered swimming at the Baths with his friends in 1951 and 1952.[2] Ivor then attended Bath Technical School. Like many former swimmers, he recalls that the water was freezing cold, but 'warmer than the river'. His friend spoke to the Superintendent about the temperature of the water, only for the Superintendent to disappear into the buildings and reappear with a kettle of boiling water which he proceeded to pour into the pool! Again, that Superintendent was likely to have been the memorable Lofty Harris.

A local swimmer in this period who was deterred by very cold water was Terry Mitchell.[3] His experience was that as a Scout, based at Southdown, he was entered into a county swimming competition at Taunton. He knew that the Taunton pool would be cold and so decided to train at the Cleveland Baths, to acclimatise himself to swimming in very cold water. He found himself standing by the main pool at the Cleveland Baths for 40 minutes, being wary of jumping in, but when he worked up the courage and jumped in, '*I had to swim fast but it was effective.*'

Another Bath resident who also swam at the Baths in her youth, in the late 1950s and early 1960s, was Sheila Stevens. Sheila, now retired, was born and brought up on the Wells Road in Bath and went to Grosvenor Secondary High School on London Road. That school was in the premises that were previously occupied by Grosvenor College in the Victorian period, when the Grosvenor students also enjoyed the use of the Cleveland Baths:

'There were about four girls and a class full of boys and we were all very keen on swimming…We were gobsmacked by it the first time we saw it (the Baths) and we were amazed by it, and the size, shape and depth of it was amazing. Beautifully maintained.'[4]

Sheila recollected that:

The Cleveland Pools pre-restoration, with forget-me-nots. Note that this view of the original buildings would have been familiar to many generations of bathers. COURTESY OF SALLY HELVEY

"One summer we just went there and it sort of became a ritual for us, and by the age of about twelve until we were sixteen, we would wait until the first of April and no matter what the weather…we would go and we would visit every night of the week including weekends, until it actually closed at the end of September for the season. I used to get home from school and would cycle to the pools. The weather was always atrocious and invariably it was only us there, I think about ten of us in total, and then at the weekends, the whole atmosphere changed, the grass bank at the back…was full of people, not so many people in the water as it was cold…We used to have great fun because there was the little pool. I think it used to close at 8.00p.m. every night. Then we would stay and help Mark, a student, clean the little pool out because he used to drain it right down.…They used ordinary water to fill up the little pool, I think they used to fill it up with a hosepipe straight from the mains so it was all clean water. I can remember one day we were helping clean out the little pool and we all fell in! We were all soaking wet and we had to cycle home!

I don't remember there being more than one attendant…at least 200 people would be there at the weekend as the bank would be crowded and they would take picnics. Obviously, the people who were there at weekends weren't all local, but they made a day out of it…It had a huge impression on me and I can still remember the beauty and simplicity of it."

The Cleveland Baths were truly a social 'hub', and memorable for many reasons. Jenny Wyatt will never forget that her husband proposed to her one day in July 1963 after he emerged from the pool – she accepted! In the following years, their children were to be regular swimmers at the Baths.

Carol Morley, who was a school girl during those years, recalled:

"I went to Bathwick school in the 1960s and Cleveland Pools (as they are known today) were on the

way home as we lived just up the hill. My mum used to take me and other friends after school for a swim, whatever the weather. I can remember swimming on rainy days and once there was a hailstorm, so we had to stay in the pool to avoid being hit by the hailstones! I recently visited Cleveland Pools after 40 years and it brought back happy memories."

Social Context

The recollections of women who enjoyed the Cleveland Baths when they were girls are resonant with social trends at that time. A national Mass Observation study carried out in 1949 interestingly showed that of the large number of girls surveyed, approximately half devoted their leisure time in summer to swimming or tennis, or both. Another study by Morgan in the same period found that approximately half of the girls responding to the questions swam in their leisure time. Public provision of pools, often including free swimming tuition, supplied a cheap and accessible activity, especially giving opportunity to working class girls (Langhamer, 2009, p.79). Generally, it has been observed that people from urban areas in this period preferred the familiar and the popular in relation to family outings (Kynaston, 2009).

Improved swimming costumes were heralded by the introduction of nylon for swimwear in the late 1950s, a stronger and smoother fabric that reduced water resistance and was quicker to dry. Two-piece suits for women that still covered the midriff were seen in the early 1950s, influenced by fabric shortages during the war, whereas later 1950s fashions included halter necks for one-piece women's costumes. The bikini had been designed in France in 1946 and became fashionable in the UK in the 1960s. Fabrics were often printed with patterns such as polka dots or later in the period, op art style designs. The Speedo company was founded and produced lightweight costumes in the new fabrics.

By the early 1960s, training of experienced swimmers focussed on interval training which consists of a series of swims of the same distance with controlled rest periods. In 1969 international swimming was regularised with the strokes allowed being reduced to freestyle (crawl), backstroke, breaststroke and butterfly. From the 1964 Olympics, individual medley races took place over the same 400m distance for both men and women. Swimming was one of the original sports when the first modern Paralympic games were held in Rome in 1960.

The city of Bath saw substantial change in the 1960s – demolition and clearance focussed on the terraced houses that had been lived in by those who had serviced the Georgian city. Clearance took place around the core of the city centre. The 37-hour working week was introduced in the late 1960s, and there were gradual increases in earnings in some categories of employment. While a week's holiday at the seaside – at, say, Weston-super-Mare or Weymouth – was possible for some families, partly reflecting the increase in car ownership, the summer season increased demands for fun and exercise that was financially within the reach of many more. The Baths provided that opportunity for families from the less advantaged areas of the city.

The Spa Committee Takes on the Baths

In 1957 there was some new thinking about the council's oversight of the baths – the Waterworks Committee agreed to approach the Spa Committee of Bath City Council about bringing the oversight of all pools under the Spa Committee. It can be speculated that the Waterworks councillors found the Baths to be a problematic and anomalous addition to their priority responsibility to supply mains water to the city. They were told in response to their approach that there was little chance of extending the present facilities at the Cleveland Baths.[5] The response from the Spa Committee councillors indicates that there was an aspiration to extend provision at the Baths and that there were likely to be insufficient funds in the Waterworks budget.

Spa Committee councillors were blunt in their assessment of the Cleveland Baths: 'It's in the wrong place'; they were filled with 'bitterly cold water'; and would cost a 'shocking amount of money to put them in order'. The comments about location and water temperature no doubt reflected the contrast with the central location of the warm-water Spa Baths. The loss on the income against expenditure for the Cleveland Baths was estimated in that period at £400 a year. Alderman Taylor, however, felt that it was the most economic amenity run by the city: 'We have had 500 to 600 people there on several occasions this year.' Alderman Burden supported him: 'If these baths are closed and we have a really hot summer, there will be an outcry from all over the city.'

Improvements were made in due course – the Bath Spa Committee did take over the responsibility for the Baths from the Waterworks Committee, running them alongside the Beau St, Royal and Cross Baths, those being located in the city centre. In 1965 the Cleveland Bath's admission cost was 9d for adults – still a reasonable cost, taking into account the council's expenditure of £700 in the previous year[6] (approximately £12,000 at today's prices).

Records show that in the early 1960s there were continuing staffing difficulties at the Baths. In Spring 1964 it was agreed that in the forthcoming season the Cleveland Baths be opened on Saturdays and Sundays only, and that the qualified swimming attendants necessary for duty at those baths be engaged from personnel at the Fire Brigade and Ambulance Service on Saturdays, and from personnel of the Spa Department on Sundays.[7] The Fire Brigade also helped by pumping out the water in the main pool at the end of the season so that it could be replaced.

The Baths could not have operated without the efforts of the Waterworks staff. Pat Payton, Alfred Davies, Bill Gay, Alan James Brown and Bert Sutton were all part of the team in the 1960s who pumped out, cleaned and whitewashed the Baths in readiness for the coming season. Detailed analysis of exterior paint on some buildings on the site indicates that they were limewashed every few years.[8]

One task was the extension of chlorination piping from the main pool to the smaller children's pool in 1960.[9] That measure would have been prompted by national fears about the polio outbreak. Concerns about polio infection were inevitably raised in the late 1950s.

Reassurance was given by the city Medical Officer of Health that the chlorination of pools such as the Cleveland Baths would prevent the potential for infection.

There were, however, warnings about swimming in the river that was thought to be polluted again by contaminated sewage.[10] So the most serious impact of the polio epidemic was on river swimming – the weir-to-weir races in the Avon were suspended again after a few years'

Photograph of Ron Gray, champion diver.
COURTESY OF HIS DESCENDANTS

revival. The proximity of the Cleveland Baths to the Avon contributed to a negative association in relation to the polio infection that could be water-borne, despite the council's reassurances that the water in the pools was substantially chlorinated.

Public demand must have eventually had sufficient impact, because a report to the Spa Committee in 1966 states that the council undertook to allocate extra funds to that committee to enable improvements to the Cleveland Baths to be carried out.[11] The aim was to improve swimming facilities and to extend opening hours. A 'shopping list' of short-term improvement to the Baths, set out as a handwritten note by Mr Rawlings, who was probably a council officer, is telling in that it includes signposting and promotion in addition to facility improvements:[12]

1   Paving instead of grass (decorated with concrete flower tubs)
2   Better signposting to the swimming pool at six points in the city
3   Provision of duckboards in the ladies' changing rooms, and separate cubicles for the gents (where plastic curtaining would be adequate)
4   Better publicity for schools and youth clubs
5   Deck chairs for hire
6   A slide in the larger pool

A new concrete floor was laid in 1967 and blue paint was applied to the main pool. Shelters dating back probably to 1910 at the east end of the main pool were removed, and a semi-circular cascade fountain that was part of the filtration system was installed in the late 1960s, at the eastern end of the main pool. The fountain and slide were loved by children and are remembered by many previous swimmers.

Wessex Water Archive Photographs – How a Mystery was Solved

The popularity of the Cleveland Baths in the 1960s as described in swimmers' memories can be seen in a set of photographs that are a valued record, showing crowds in the summer season – adults and children alike having lots of fun. The photographs were taken by Baths attendants who were employees of Wessex Water, the successor to the municipal Water Board. The collection was transferred in recent years from the Wessex Water archives to the Museum of Bath At Work.

One of the 1960s photographs showed an athletic young man performing a handstand on a diving board. The image became known amongst volunteers in the last decade as 'Handstand Man'. It was often shown at events and in a 'Where Are They Now?' feature in the *Bath Chronicle*, in the hope that he would be identified by family or friends.

The local press feature was successful in that the Gray family came forward – their father Ron Gray was then discovered to be the mysterious Handstand Man. He was a champion diver with the Bath Dolphin Swimming Club. In a fitting gesture, on the Heritage Open Days weekend in September 2014, on which over 1,300 people took a look at the unique pools site, Ron's family were presented with framed prints of his handstand.

The memories of swimmers included in this chapter and the next vividly illustrate the social importance of the Baths, to meet friends, make new like-minded friends and enjoy family get-togethers. We can envisage everyone relaxing for hours when they were blessed with good summer weather, in the lovely riverside setting. There was a supervisor and expectations of social behaviour, but no regimentation. That approach in a leisure facility enabled personal development – building confidence while gaining social and swimming skills. Unsurprisingly, the Pools are held in high regard by those who swam there – remembering cherished leisure time spent at such a special place. The next chapter examines the last decades of the history of the Cleveland Baths before they closed in the 1980s.

Aerial view of the Cleveland Pools when it was a trout farm. COURTESY OF JOHN DAGGER

Chapter 10

The 1970s and 1980s – End of an Era and Closure

'It is something that you pass by and didn't think of, and then we went down there and our jaws dropped, it was just amazing, it's this incredible place and it was like a secret location, a secret garden, a secret water garden…We went down there and we swam there every available time we could and stayed until the early evenings or whatever time they closed.'[1]

This chapter covers the period from the 1970s to 1984, when the Baths were finally closed for swimming. It will describe the experiences of some of those who swam in the Baths, using their own reminiscences. The final section of the chapter examines the competition posed by the warm waters of the Leisure Centre to cold-water swimming at the Baths. A profile of the last Superintendent, John Dagger, is also included in this chapter – he was a very accomplished swimmer and trainer, contributing much, much more than a purely supervisory role. Large numbers of people living in Bath and the surrounding area learned how to swim with his encouragement and direction.

Swimmers' Recollections and Reflections

One previous swimmer at the Baths recalled that:[2]
"I lived in a house on Cleveland Row in the early 70s that backed onto the Cleveland Baths. Summers were glorious in the evening when they were closed…we used to get over the wall at the bottom of the garden and swim in the freezing water! Memories!"

Many people remember swimming in the Baths in the 1970s and 1980s, and their reminiscences provide valuable insights into the experience of swimming there in that period. It is not intended that those quoted here should be seen as a representative sample; rather that their reminiscences give us a more direct understanding of the impact of the Baths on the lives of these young swimmers, in the context of their lives overall. Even more importantly, their recollections bring to life their experiences as swimmers by conveying their feelings or impressions and capturing details of everyday life.

For instance, many children still wore knitted swimming suits. An ex-swimmer reminisced that in his youth: *'I used to swim in a pair of trunks knitted by my grandmother! In fact, I had my first Speedos when I was about eleven. I used to swim so fast when I had them because there was no*

An example of men's woollen swimming trunks. COURTESY SALLY HELVEY

drag from those woollen trunks![3] The older generation will remember knitted swimming trunks, more often machine-knitted rather than hand-knitted, but still heavy and dragging when wet.

Some of those who swam in the Baths in the 1970s were part of a long family tradition. Mick Ringham's father and uncles swam in the Baths and he had heard stories of his grandfather, who was a keen swimmer living in Widcombe, swimming in the Avon and on *'high days and holidays sneaking in to the Baths. In those days (1920s or 1930s) there was no tuition'.* Mick recollects that his father didn't speak much about the Baths as they were taken for granted, 'part of the wallpaper', but when Mick and his wife returned to Bath after living in Cornwall for a period, they discovered the Baths for themselves:

"It was fantastic and people would take their picnics down…they served ice cream and lollies, but it was pretty dilapidated then and this was about the late 1970s, early 80s. You could see it was a faded beauty but it was just great and the pool was deep and there were all these families about just having picnics and they would spend the whole day there, and the kids' holidays were just amazing, there was no need to go away.

The kiddies' pool was fully operational, and when our kids started to come down we would take them and take a picnic, and we would spend about three hours there and just talk and read the papers, and, of course, there was the grass bank and that's where all the people would sort of congregate and they would treat it as their own garden with a pool in it."[4]

It is unsurprising that those swimmers took the Baths for granted, as the site was there from their early childhood and previous generations had swum there. The sheer pleasure of outdoor swimming and socialising was what drew them to the Baths, rather than the relatively unpromoted heritage importance as one of a cluster of historic sites in the city of Bath.

One young swimmer who had no idea of the Baths' historic importance was Stephanie Adams, who currently works at the Bath Record Office:

'I think I must have been one of the last people to swim in the Cleveland Baths before they closed to the public. We had moved to Bathwick, just around the corner from the Baths, one summer in the late 1970s. I remember being in the back garden and hearing shouts

A boy having fun on the fountain in 1973. COURTESY BATH IN TIME © BATH AND NORTH EAST SOMERSET COUNCIL

and laughter every afternoon and my mother telling us that it must be coming from the swimming baths…it sounded as though everyone was having quite a party there every day, so eventually I went up with my brother to investigate.

I remember sitting down on the edge of the pool for the first time, putting my feet in and drawing them out again with a loud gasp as the water was so cold. It took ages for me to get right down into the water and the situation was not made any easier by my brother 'accidentally' splashing me with cold water whenever he had the opportunity!

We went up many times that summer as there was always such a fun atmosphere and everyone seemed to be having such a good time, but I don't think I ever really got used to the temperature of that water…'

Richard and Debbie Mower, who now live in Yate, recollect that they:

'…just always knew that the pools were there; it's not something that we were ever told about, we just knew they were there…We both lived within walking distance so we used to walk there…It was unique really and it was a great place to go and you meet up with your friends and you spend the whole day…You had to pay to go in, it wasn't a lot though…that was the amount you paid for the whole day.'

Richard thought that *'it was just really amazing and especially for me. It was just a good place to meet everyone when the weather was good, and 1974–76 were good summers.'* Debbie recalled: *'I can remember going with my mother and sister, and I would go swimming with a group, but yes I think my mum used to take me and my sisters there.'* Both remembered that *'there were lots of adults back then…parents with younger children, and teenagers on their own.'*

Both Richard and Debbie thought that it would be brilliant if the Pools were reopened: *'We would take our grandchildren. It would have a successful future…If you've got the weather and if everyone knew about it then they would enjoy it.'*[5]

The Last Superintendent – John Dagger

The last Baths Superintendent and experienced swimming instructor, John Dagger, was appointed by the Bath City Council's Waterworks Department in 1975. The job title was Sports Officer: Pools, his counterpart being Sports Officer: Dry. His partner Jenny was a receptionist at the new Leisure Centre, which opened in that same year. John's experience was invaluable – his career in Bath had started when he became a pool attendant at the Beau St Baths in the city in 1956 at the age of 22. Prior to that, John, like a number of other Cleveland Baths superintendents before him, served in the Royal Navy, where he taught swimming to new recruits at the Davenport Dockyards.

John Dagger greets Norma Heath at a Swimmers Reunion in 2016 – they had not met for 37 years. Norma ran the kiosk at the Cleveland Baths and remembered Commander Forsberg training in the pool. COURTESY OF SALLY HELVEY

The Sports and Leisure Centre on North Parade, Bath, showing building in progress in 1972.
COURTESY BATH IN TIME © BATH AND NORTH EAST SOMERSET COUNCIL

He had been the swimming instructor for the Bath Dolphin Swimming Club at the Beau St Baths and gained his qualifications with the Club – a continuation of the link between the Cleveland Baths and the Dolphin Club that dated back for nearly a hundred years.

So, John brought experience in teaching swimming to the Cleveland Baths. While he was working there, John's qualifications led to an appointment with the Bristol and District Lifesaving Society, whose catchment area included Bath. He was soon promoted to be on the Regional Executive for the National Lifesaving Society, becoming a judge of competitions at national and international level, and an Olympic standard judge of Lifesaving examinations.

In the 1970s John's achievements were acknowledged when he was awarded Commonwealth recognition badges by the Queen on three occasions for his outstanding contributions to swimming coaching and teaching.

The Baths' Closure

In 1975 the Baths were formally listed by English Heritage as a Grade 1 heritage asset. This listing meant that in broad terms, the Baths were considered to be of special architectural and historical importance. Listing means that the heritage has to be taken into account when there are planning applications for changes or development. Despite gaining this status, in the late 1970s and early 1980s the Baths were threatened with closure by the City Council. The primary concern for the councillors was the opening of the council's Sports and Leisure Centre on the south side of North Parade in 1975. From the outset, the Centre was understandably popular, with its indoor warm-water swimming pool, which could be used in all weathers, and its modern amenities. Another well-known public baths in Bath was closed for good – the Beau St Baths, tepid, mineral-water-fed baths on the site of what is now the Thermae Bath Spa. The Cleveland Baths still had many individual loyal bathers in the late 1970s, as demonstrated by a petition to keep them open, which gained over a thousand signatures in 1978.

In the wider north-east Somerset area, towns with smaller populations supported a range of indoor and outdoor pools that were valued by local communities, but these also came under threat during the 1970s. The Midsomer Norton open-air pool at Welton was open in the summer seasons of the 1970s. The Victoria Jubilee indoor baths at Frome had a longer history. They had been opened in 1901 and were built in a converted iron foundry. As was the case in Bath, there was an emphasis here on swimming lessons – nearly every child in

Summer splash at the Cleveland Baths, 1983.
COURTESY BATH IN TIME © BATH AND NORTH EAST SOMERSET COUNCIL

Frome was said to have been taught to swim at these baths by the time of their closure. The Frome baths were also affected by the opening of a new local indoor sports centre near to Frome College and they were closed in 1975.

It was inevitable that the availability of cheap package holidays also adversely affected the public's view of outdoor swimming in the UK: 'Foreign travel to warmer climes', once the privilege of the wealthy, raised expectations that an unheated pool on a blustery day could simply no longer fulfil. As one regular lido user recalled, '*At the time, a water temperature of 60 degrees Fahrenheit seemed normal. We didn't know any better. But later, once the family had been to Spain, they certainly didn't want to go into that again.*' (Smith, 2005, pp.23-24)

By the 1970s and 1980s lidos in England had fallen out of favour with government and national sport advisory authorities. Heated indoor pools with nationally recognised standard dimensions were supported, and attracted investment. Between 1972 and 1981, over 400 new sports centres were built in the UK, typically providing swimming, badminton or squash courts and gym facilities (Clarke and Critcher, 1985). The University of Bath opened its first indoor pool in 1974, funding being awarded in 1994 for the current 50-metre Olympic standard pool.

Local swimmers still wore knitted bathing suits, in the early 1970s, before the lighter stretch fabrics such as Lycra fibre or nylon/elastane became more affordable. Men's swimwear designs became more diverse and reasonably priced, ranging from long cotton boxer style shorts to brief trunks. Swimming teaching as a facility offered by local pools was well established and prevalent. More competent swimmers participated in competitions at various levels.

The proposed closure of the Cleveland Baths was a blow to those who enjoyed outdoor swimming as a valued leisure activity. Richard and Debbie Mower remember that:

'When we learnt about it closing we were quite shocked…I know there was a great feeling of loss when it did go, but over time people forgot it and the weeds grew over like a fairy-tale castle, and all of a sudden it's forgotten.'[6]

Attempts to Reopen or Repurpose the Baths

In 1981–82 there was a private attempt by an individual, Jolyon Trimingham, to reopen the Baths. He was granted a five-year lease in 1982, opened the Baths for swimming that summer and aimed to secure cash to support the initiative. This was, unfortunately, not successful, as he was let down by a prospective funder. Sue Lucy was involved in helping out at the Baths in that period:

'My friends and I opened the main pool to the public, hired inflatables for the children to play on and had 'new romantic' bands play there on a couple of evenings…I never got paid for any of this help – it was a labour of love and a chance to do something positive.

We used the old wire baskets for clothes in the changing rooms, sold ice lollies and drinks and had a lifeguard/pool attendant to look after the water cleaning and safety of the general public while in the pool…We used rather tatty plastic tables and chairs around the pool for people to have refreshments or just sit and chat.

My son remembers having lots of fun playing in the large pool that summer with other children, and people would lay around on their towels listening to music or families would bring picnics and make a day of it…It was a wonderful place to be. We also had dreams of getting funds to build a jetty at the river so that people could arrive by boat, but this never got off the ground.'

After Jolyon Trimingham's prospective funder failed to supply the necessary investment, the Baths closed again. Despite that failure to gain funding, other attempts were made to maintain open-air swimming at the Baths, even if it was on a more restricted basis. Brian Popay, who became a senior performer with the Natural Theatre Company, was one of those who tried to open up the Baths again. He moved into Cleveland Row in about 1980, and stayed there until 1990 in what was then called the Bath Housing Co-op.

'Myself and a few other people came up with the idea of reopening it on a summer basis, so we got permission from the council and we cleaned it all out and had to empty the pool, and it was fed by a spring from the hill, so we had to pump that out and scrub it and paint it, and reopened in the summer and had it running for two years.'

In common with many swimmers, Brian remembers the shock of the cold water: *'It was absolutely freezing and hard going, and you have to be ready to be really cold and you have to enjoy that, the water came straight from the spring.'* He remembers that:

'I think it was 1985 or 1986, and the summer happened to be very hot and sunny so they were open every day…Loads of people came, it's not that well known because it's hidden and out of the way, but it

attracted a regular crowd…there's no parking so that was another problem. We had a nominal sum to come in…I think about fifty pence at most, it was cheap…we had food and ice cream down there…it was a lovely day out, and it was really packed, it was surprising how many people could fit onto the grass bank.

When we got hold of it the first time, we had parties down there and had film shows in the pool. We had a friend who had a film club and we would take projectors down there. We painted all the walls in the pools white. We would have evening parties down there while we were carrying out work…It was just for the people who worked there to encourage them to continue with the work. Just to celebrate how far we got; it must have taken us about a week to fix it up.

We started an adventure playground in the 70s so we knew a lot of people and locals, and we had been involved in the Snowhill young people's scene, we had quite a lot of connections in that area…So, people came and enjoyed the finished product with their families.[7]

When the Baths were first closed for swimming, John Dagger, the last Superintendent, moved into the cottage at the centre of the mini-crescent of changing rooms and opened a café where cream teas could be enjoyed, in the floored-over Ladies' Pool. The Baths reopened for a year in 1984, in a period when the Sports Centre was closed, and again were popular.

After the Leisure Centre reopened, John Dagger opened a Trout Farm on the site with his partner Jenny and he taught swimming at the Centre, going on to become the Assistant Director of Leisure Services for the council later in the 1980s. The Trout Farm was relatively successful and operated until 2002. Many Bathonians have memories of buying trout there, including Jack Sparrow. He recalls that customers were offered a rod, to catch their own trout. That was an attraction, and he returned several times as '*it was quite entertaining to fish for your supper, so to speak.*' Jack remembers that one year, the river flooded into the pool and the fish swam out to the river.

With his partner Jenny, John Dagger's other initiatives on the site included the introduction of koi carp into the smaller upper pool and even the construction of an oriental 'willow pattern'-style bridge over that pool. The carp were provided by a Japanese resident of Bath who had brought them from the trout pools owned by Emperor Hirohito. Weekends were busy and four lifeguards were deployed, acknowledging the depth and cold temperature of the pool.

A postscript in relation to John Dagger and Jenny is that they have lived in the area since the 1980s, marrying on St. Lucia in 2018. John has been a regular visitor to swimmers' reunions and other events at the Pools in recent years, welcomed by many ex-swimmers who remember him.[8]

The closure of the Cleveland Pools for swimming is unsurprising when there was a new indoor warm-water swimming facility in the centre of Bath that offered year-round use. In terms of financial investment, the council prioritised the Centre's warm pool. This, combined with the relative lack of wider public awareness of the age of the Pools, their remarkable history and their national heritage implications, led to their neglect – until a few community activists initiated the campaign to save them. The next chapter explores the fourteen-year campaign to restore the Pools for future generations to enjoy.

Pre-restoration view of the Cleveland Pools in 2018. COURTESY OF SALLY HELVEY

Chapter 11

Campaign and Restoration

This chapter sets out a summary of the sustained campaign to restore the Cleveland Pools. An account is given of the concerted work to raise awareness and to secure the vital capital funds, resulting in major restoration work, which started at last in 2021.

Any campaign that progresses from lobbying by a few dedicated community activists to directing a multi-million-pound restoration project will undergo huge challenges in making the leaps in development that are crucial. That transition is never smooth. People with widely differing skills and experience have to pull together, despite their varying perspectives and vision. It would be impossible to provide a comprehensive narrative of the fifteen-year effort, so instead we have chosen to include recollections contributed by a range of individuals who had a role in the sustained push for restoration of the Pools.

A Community-Led Campaign

In common with many community projects across the UK, the restoration of the Pools was first triggered by a very few local people in Bath who had the vision and energy to launch a campaign 'against the odds', in the face of enormous barriers. One of the first community campaigners, who is now the Honorary President of the Cleveland Pools Trust, was Ann Dunlop. Ann and her husband came to live in Bath in 1980. They settled in a house where the Kensington Meadows was just beyond the rear of their garden.

It was only when the Pools (then known as the Cleveland Baths) were advertised on the open market that Ann 'fully realised that they were there' – located on the opposite bank of the river from Kensington Meadows. Ann took advantage of the public viewing days for prospective buyers, as did Roger Houghton and Janice Dreisbach. All three of them were active on community issues and would become founder trustees of the charity. Ann and Janice, who lived on the Snow Hill Estate, were involved in the local community partnership that was concerned with issues affecting the London Rd area, and Roger was able to give advice from his experience with planning issues.

In 2004 the Baths site was marketed on behalf of Bath & North East Somerset Council for a sale cost of £400,000. The 2006 Cleveland Pools Feasibility Study[1] commented that this was a remarkable amount to request of a buyer, given the limited extent of useable accommodation and in the light of the physical, environmental, planning and heritage constraints of the site. At the time of publication of the Feasibility Study, the council was still seeking

Pre-restoration photograph showing the steps to the deep end of the main pool. COURTESY OF SALLY HELVEY

offers for the property. The site was advertised as being 0.75 acres in extent and was offered with a 150-year lease. Prospective purchasers would see in the sale information pack[2] the rather blunt but accurate understatement: 'The pools are somewhat dilapidated.'

The campaigners' main objective was to prevent the Pools from being sold to a private developer and to open the site for the people of Bath to enjoy. Other people who had viewed the site were prospective developers and residents of nearby Hampton Row. The local press proved to be supportive to the community campaigners at the time of the proposed sale of the site, as were all of the local community members who lived close to the Pools.

After the Pools were advertised for the second time on the open market, Roger Houghton wrote to all members of Bath & North East Somerset Council, making the case against the sale of this remarkable heritage site.

The Early Stages of the Campaign

A well-attended public meeting was organised, generating donations to the campaign, with an accompanying petition to raise public awareness. Local councillors David Dixon and Colin Darracott were encouraging to the campaigners. It was decided to set up a charity after David Dunlop proposed the initiative at a meeting of the Bath Society, and the Cleveland Pools Trust was registered in 2005 in the form of a company limited by guarantee. The change of name from the Cleveland Baths to the Cleveland Pools was introduced by trustees at that time – their purpose was to clearly differentiate the Pools from the Spa Bath complex in the city centre and the indoor baths at the Sports Centre.

An interesting proposal that was put forward in this period was made by Jem Tayle and Maggie Lyons, holistic therapists who wished to set up healing therapy provision in the unique natural environment at the Pools. This was not the right time to develop such a project, but it anticipated a theme of well-being that was to increasingly reflect the concerns of supporters of the Pools.

In those significant early years of the Trust's development, there were just three trustees whose focus was to campaign for the recognition of the Pools' value to the local community in Bath. By 2006 there were over 60 fee-paying 'Friends' and 600 registered supporters. However, Bath City Council generally was not supportive of the campaign to save the Pools, having previously agreed that their preferred option was to sell them to a private buyer. An alternative option for the council was that its partner company who ran the indoor baths at the Sports Centre should take on the management of the Pools; the Trust explored other options, such as involving the Landmark Trust.

Under the auspices of the Bath Society, who were concerned about what might happen to the Pools, an application was made to upgrade the Pools' listing from Grade II to II*, which was awarded in 2006.[3] Grade II listed buildings are protected by national legislation, in that they are classified as being of special interest and cannot be altered or demolished without permission from the local planning authority. Most buildings constructed between 1700 and 1850 are listed, the purpose being to protect them for future generations. The Grade II* listing would make it much easier to attract major funding for conservation or restoration.

Janice Dreisbach accessed the resources at the Bath Central Library and the Bath Record Office to research the history of the Pools in the Georgian period, with a view to producing an illustrated booklet showing some of the main points of the history (Dreisbach, 2008). The Cleveland Pools' trustees badgered the council to allow the site to be open to the public on the Heritage Open Days that are usually held for a few days in September each year. This was first allowed in 2007, and has been organised by trustees and volunteers every year since, with large numbers of people from Bath and the wider area coming along to explore the site.

Analysis and recording of the conservation implications of the unique Georgian 'standing heritage' represented by the Pools was vitally important. It was fortunate that Ainslie Ensom, who was studying for her Master of Science degree in Historic Building Conservation at the University of Bath, chose to carry out a detailed conservation study of the Pools in 2008. Ainslie went on to work in the field of heritage consultancy, joined the Cleveland Pools Trust in 2011 and updated the Conservation Statement[4] in 2012 so that it could constitute an essential submission as part of the first funding bid to the Heritage Lottery Fund (HLF). Ainslie's vision for the Pools' restoration was that every attention should be given to conservation principles, with the original buildings being preserved authentically, generating a 'low key' experience for the visitor.

Campaigners forged ahead as best they could, with minimal resources and without the backing of the council as the site owner. Street collections were held to gather funds and to raise awareness. The involvement of influential individuals with other perspectives and experience gradually led to fresh momentum for the long restoration campaign.

Professional Input from a Notable Architect Practice

Another supportive community activist, Alex Schlesinger, was a friend of George Ferguson, co-founder of the award-winning Ferguson Mann architect practice based in Bristol, who was to be elected as the first Mayor of Bristol in 2012. He enabled Chris Balme, one of his experienced practice architects, to view the site and to give time to assist the newly forming Trust. This was a key contribution, as it is customary that an architect might draw in and lead a team of other professionals such as engineers and quantity surveyors.

Chris was to go on to lead the professional and technical team that worked on the Pools' development grant applications.

Sarah Ball, a 'Heritage At Risk' specialist architect at English Heritage, became involved. The new Trust put in their first grant application to English Heritage – made possible by the Grade II* listing, as that met a key criteria for funding. A grant was given for work to empty the main pool, in order to carry out the physical investigation needed to assess the state of the base and walls of the pool. English Heritage (now Heritage England) was to allocate vital grants over the next fifteen years, with the objective of filling gaps in funding, particularly to resource investigation of the historic buildings, and to give impetus to the restoration project. English Heritage also took part in 'behind the scenes' meetings with Bath & North East Somerset Council, bringing their authority and heritage experience to influence those discussions. A smaller-scale funder over many years was the Architectural Heritage Fund, which provided valuable advice, drawing on national experience.

Modern photograph pre-restoration showing the steps into the empty Cleveland Baths upper pool. COURTESY OF SALLY HELVEY

The Cleveland Pools were recorded on the Heritage At Risk Register, which is managed by English Heritage, and the stated condition was 'very bad, priority A'. The purpose of the Register is to tell communities about the condition of their local neighbourhood, to encourage them to become actively involved in looking after precious heritage, and to reassure them that any public funding goes to the most needy and urgent cases. English Heritage contributed significant grants for technical assessments to enable the Options Appraisal to be prepared, and also provided grants to fund essential maintenance and safety-related work on site.

Some council staff sought to be constructive in their approach to the Cleveland Pools. For example, Hayley Ponsford, an estates surveyor in Property Services, recommended an approach to Peter Davenport, a senior consultant at Cotswold Archaeology: that approach was fruitful in resulting in the production of the first archaeological evaluation of the Pools' historic buildings.[5]

A role that became increasingly important to fill was the input of business sector advice, informed by a successful track record in the commercial sector. The Bath-based individual who stepped forward to fill that gap was Trevor Osborne, who had an established high profile in the property development sphere.

A Business Perspective

Trevor Osborne became aware of the Cleveland Pools in the period after they were advertised for sale – his attention was drawn to the Pools by the Bath MP at that time, Don Foster, who suggested that the Trust needed to be guided by both commercial considerations and historic building conservation. Trevor was keen to see the development of the Pools' potential and agreed to direct Chris Balme, architect at the Ferguson Mann practice, and to guide the widening role of the Trust. He chaired the steering group for some time – that group included trustees and professionals.

Trevor's experience informed his view that the Pools could only be sustainable if they had an attractive 'offer' that was acceptable to visitors to Bath, including heritage visitors. He recommended contemporary design to complement heritage architecture and advocated that all visitors to the Pools, including Bath residents, should be able to expect a 'five star' experience. Trevor identified capacity building as a priority and enabled Jo Booker, his Business PA, to become an active trustee, offering her own expertise.

Trevor was a catalyst in that he involved The Princes Regeneration Trust, a national organisation dedicated to regenerating often neglected historic buildings to bring them into use to meet social objectives, with community support. Trevor persuaded the Director, Ros Kerslake (now director of the National Heritage Lottery Fund), to take over the leadership of the steering group from him.

Following his work with the Cleveland Pools Trust, Trevor moved on to other projects in Bath and beyond. Most recently his company has restored the Georgian Buxton Crescent Hotel & Spa in Derbyshire, listed as Grade 1 and stated by the Chief Executive Officer of Historic England to be 'the most significant restoration project of the decade'. Trevor Osborne considers that the drive to secure the prospective restoration of the Cleveland Pools is an impressive achievement.

Key Support at National Level

The co-ordinating role and experience offered by The Prince's Regeneration Trust enabled the Steering Group to be supported and developed for many years, overseeing the workshop which enabled the Trust to develop a shared vision of the future of the Pools – essential to making real progress.Ultimately, they assisted with the initial application for funding to the HLF. The steering group involved individuals such as Tony Crouch, World Heritage Manager for the City of Bath World Heritage Site, and Keith McCombie, from the council's Property Services, to complement the roles of trustees and the professional and technical team. Ros Kerslake introduced her sister Ruth Kerslake to meetings of the steering group, as Ruth had considerable experience on the community leisure trust that successfully restored and managed the Arundel Lido – a popular community pool.

Ros Kerslake, who is now the Chief Executive of the National Heritage Lottery Fund, recalls that when she became involved, the local council did not take seriously the future of the Pools as a community-run project. There appeared to be an assumption on the part of the council that they would have to take back full responsibility for the semi-derelict site. Ros's driving vision was that the Cleveland Pools should be reinstated to their original use as a public open-air swimming pool, with an integral focus on its national heritage status. She wrote the bid document to the Council, setting out the Trust's vision for its future, and secured their agreement to supporting the community-led project.

Her concerns, drawing on her experience, included the need to build local capacity and the skills needed to oversee a major restoration scheme, the need to assess whether the restoration of swimming was viable and the requirement for a credible business plan to be constructed. Her view was that the Pools must have a 'cultural offer' that incorporated its unique history and the attraction of its riverside setting. Relative to other heritage restoration projects, this was a very challenging one. Access was one of the most complex features to tackle, given the very limited entrance to the site and local area parking restrictions. The Trust, through Ros and a number of its staff including Fred Taggart (who introduced the author to the project) and Manuela Belle, continued to actively support the project until funding enabled a full-time project manager to be appointed, and thereafter remained as a 'critical friend'.

The determination of the steering group led to a detailed Options Appraisal and Business Plan being commissioned by the Cleveland Pools Trust in 2010/11, with the help and support of English Heritage and The Prince's Regeneration Trust. These documents included a costing framework that supported the Trust's conviction that the Cleveland Pools had a viable future as a community-led project. This was the necessary springboard for the first application to the HLF to resource the necessary development work needed, before a major application could be made for restoration funding.

The commitment of national heritage organisations to the Pools' restoration partly reflected the marked return of enthusiasm for outdoor swimming:

'It has been said that the return of the lido is a result of rising summer temperatures, or the purported fact that British are not as wealthy as they once were and unable to take summer holidays abroad. The truth is simpler: they have always been cherished as community resources...and their temporary demise was the anomaly.'[6]

Bidding for the Development Grant

The Trust first applied to the HLF for a development grant in April 2012. That grant would fund a technical and professional team involving architects, engineers, surveyors and other specialists to carry out all of the assessments on site needed to prepare a bid for a major capital grant to restore the pools for public use. Vital voluntary project management assistance was given by Rob Harding (ex-English Heritage project manager) in 2011-12 and again in 2014 with regard to the resubmission. Rob saw that HLF funding, if it came to fruition, would not only save an unusual heritage asset, but it would also bestow *'a near-*

magical place for people to visit and enjoy'. To that end, he would *'want the adopted scheme to be enthusiastically supported by all involved and to be financially viable to build and run'*. The HLF was particularly interested in the bid in 2012, but requested that more preparation be done by trustees before a further application was made.

Encouraged by HLF's clear interest in the Pools, the Trust took forward action to strengthen leadership and to draw on experience of developing major projects, public relations and marketing, business skills, accountancy and linking with schools. An event for business contacts was organised in July 2013, sponsored by The Bath Spa Hotel – the Guest of Honour was Sharron Davies, an ex-Olympic swimmer who is a Patron and active ambassador for the Pools' restoration project.

By 2014, Bath & North East Somerset Council, the site owner, agreed, subject to a successful HLF application, to grant a 150-year lease of the site to the Cleveland Pools Trust. Full planning approval was also given. A capital funding contribution was committed by the council – a critical decision, as it would not have been feasible to submit a bid for a major grant to HLF without that council commitment. Important steps forward also included completion of a business plan, other fundraising and an influx of formal letters of support for the Pools' restoration from a wide array of local businesses, city heritage organisations and individuals.

Securing the Restoration Grant

The development grant from HLF was awarded to the Cleveland Pools Trust in 2014 – the appointed Project Director, Christopher Heath, put in place a project design team co-ordinated by Provolio management consultancy, based in Bristol. The team,

Volunteers meeting the public on Heritage Open Day 2016. COURTESY OF THE CLEVELAND POOLS TRUST

led by Christopher and the Trust, embarked on a complex work programme. Consultation on the final design for the restored site involved local residents, the appointed project design team including business planners, architects/landscape architects, interpretation consultants, engineers, natural pool consultants, wildlife experts; the Environment Agency, local council, Historic England, local interest groups and a variety of successful comparator open-air pools. One of the leading specialist architects was Peter Carey, a dedicated and talented conservation architect from Donald Insall Associates, who had worked on the Thermae Spa design, amongst other notable UK projects. Peter sadly died in 2018 and is much missed by his colleagues and clients.

For the Trust members overseeing the challenging

development programme, a particular highlight during this period was the series of very well-attended events held in the summer of 2015 to mark the Pools' Bicentenary. One of the programme events was a fun fashion show of historic bathing costumes, organised and modelled by Bath Spa University students.

The experience of bidding to HLF for the major restoration grant, totalling £4.6 million, was a rollercoaster of very substantial effort and some setbacks. The first bid was rejected in 2017 with a request for strengthening of aspects of the application. Further work followed, led by the Trust, resulting in success – HLF board-level agreement to award the capital grant, in December 2018.

A fundamental criteria for HLF was the community-based, independent status of the Cleveland Pools Trust. On a national level:

'Historic pools have seen hard times and many have been lost or are now threatened. At the same time, there are many examples of historic pools being saved and thriving. Many lidos, and an increasing number of indoor pools, have been rescued by local residents, with inspiring community campaigns active across the country.' (Pusill and Wilkins, 2019, p.15)

A Concerted Volunteering Effort

For most of the restoration campaign, no less than 60 volunteers have been engaged with the Cleveland Pools in a number of vital roles. At the time of the first development funding bid to HLF, more than 90 volunteers were active in site maintenance, fundraising, supporting events, giving talks to local interest groups, guiding visitors around the site and liaising with the community. The eagerness of hundreds of young swimmers was seen in the fundraising Swimathon event held in February 2017, when 600 swimmers from eight swimming schools and clubs took part – the Pools' Paralympian patron, Stephanie Millward, inspired children taking part in the initiative.

Volunteers' badges designed in 2021. COURTESY OF MATTHEW CROFT

This detailed history of the Pools would not have been possible without the research contribution of committed volunteers who were enthralled by the process of discovering features of the Pools' vibrant 200-year history. The third Patron of the Pools has contributed essential guidance on how to put together and present that history – she is June Hannam, Emeritus Professor of Modern History at the University of the West of England. Supported students from both Bath Spa University and Bath University have contributed intensive work on projects such as oral history interviewing and historical research.

Volunteers have been key to the success of the annual Heritage Open Days. Visitors, including many ex-swimmers, thronged to the Pools site during a few days each September for the national initiative. Over one five-year period in the 2000s, more than 4,000 adults and children visited and made pleas for the restoration of swimming.

In common with other community-run projects, the Cleveland Pools Trust has been, and continues to be, reliant on volunteers to take the span of planned activity forward. The Trust had no paid staff until 2014, when the first paid Project Director, Christopher Heath, was appointed.

Structuring the Trustee Team

The prospective restoration of the Cleveland Pools was, and continues to be, a major responsibility. The trustee team in holding that responsibility necessarily had to reflect proven skills including management and oversight of other heritage projects, running leisure facilities, managing large budgets and public relations. The necessary range of specialist perspectives inevitably means that differences of policy emphasis need to be mediated to engender a single forward direction.

Ina Harris got involved as a volunteer, shortly after she attended a Larkhall History Society talk in 2012 by Linda Watts, on the history of the Pools. She became a trustee quite quickly and continues as a trustee, in the role of Deputy Chair of the Board. Her commitment reflects her enjoyment of being part of this very special restoration project, with its sense of common purpose. She values the emphasis on the Pools being promoted and available to the wider public, complemented by outreach work with relatively disadvantaged people.

Bidding for development funding in 2014 was strengthened by further new trustees joining the board. One of those new trustees was Tom Boden. Tom was the project manager working for the Bath Preservation Trust and was part of the team delivering the HLF-funded project to enhance the visitor experience at No.1 Royal Crescent. Tom was a long-term resident of Bath, a keen swimmer and was aware of the 'hidden, amazing' Cleveland Pools, 'the oldest surviving outdoor pool in the UK'. For him, it was a wonderful idea to have publicly accessible outdoor swimming in a heritage setting.

Tom recollects that it was a fascinating experience to work with the diverse group of trustees. Tom Boden's

The Boules for the Pools team, involving trustees and volunteers, ready for the fund-raising Bath Boules tournament, 2017. COURTESY OF SALLY HELVEY

A young Heritage Open Day visitor with her picture of Captain Evans. COURTESY OF SALLY HELVEY

vision for the Pools encompassed their place in the UNESCO World Heritage city, linking with the other significant features of 'the story of the waters of Bath', including the Thermae Spa. The Pools site embodies several of the Outstanding Universal Values for which Bath was designated as a World Heritage Site in 1987, notably Georgian architecture and social history.

An inevitable preoccupation for heritage interests in the city of Bath is the strategy for recovery from the huge impacts of the coronavirus pandemic on tourism, whether internationally or within the UK. One consideration is that the restored Cleveland Pools will have a part to play in ensuring that visitors to the city can enjoy a broader experience during a visit lasting several days. In addition to experiencing the Roman Baths and the Royal Crescent, they will be able to swim outdoors in a heritage setting, optionally with access to the Pools via a riverboat leisurely travelling past the willows on the Avon, or by way of a cycle ride on the nearby canal towpath.

Tom Boden was to become the General Manager of the Bath area National Trust and in due course he had to relinquish his Pools trustee role due to the scale of his responsibilities. Trustees in 2021 remarkably include two of the original campaigners, Ann Dunlop and Roger Houghton, and the Trustee Board is chaired by Paul Simons, who has considerable experience of heritage restoration and a focus on historic spas in Europe. They oversee the roles of paid staff recruited in 2019 to take forward the restoration project: the Project Director; Anna Baker and the Community and Volunteer Support Officer; Sam Grief, working with Jo Fairburn in a key administrative support role.

~~~~~~~~~~~~~~~~~~~~~~~~~~~~~~~~~~

CLEVELAND POOLS

This history of the Cleveland Pools has aimed to generate a fully researched narrative of the social history of the Pools. The Pools are highly significant on a number of levels, ranging from the personal history of people living in and around Bath, to international consideration in the context of the World Heritage Site. This book demonstrates that the Georgian legacy of the Cleveland Pools was followed by 200 years of fascinating social change. Through successive decades, there was plainly an enduring public enjoyment of swimming, love of fun and avid attention to displays of skill. That opportunity for exercise and delight in personal well-being will be more vital than ever when society emerges from the coronavirus pandemic. This treasured and totally unique asset is now subject to renewal and relaunch – preserving and prolonging the Pools' very special place within the history of the city of Bath and the UK.

Artist's impression of the restored Cleveland Pools. CLEVELAND POOLS TRUST COLLECTION

References

Chapter 1
1. Hembry, 1997
2. Reid, 1795 & 1798; Currie, 1797; Jackson, 1808
3. Floyer, 1715, p.19
4. Lykke Syse, 2010, p.49
5. Crebbin-Bailey, Harcup & Harrington, 2004
6. Wesley, 1747, IV 10
7. Strutt, 1801, p.74
8. Lykke Syse, 2010, p.50
9. Lykke Syse, 2010, p.36
10. Tomory, 2017, p.225
11. Elliott, 2019, p.141
12. Hembry, 1997, pp.2 & 54
13. Neale, 1981
14. Sheard, 2000, pp.65-66
15. Hembry, 1997, p.3
16. Hembry, 1997, p.6
17. Neale, 1981
18. Borsay, 2000
19. Borsay, 2000
20. Knight, 2013
21. Barratts map of Bath, published 1818, Bath Record Office
22. Neale, 1981

Chapter 2
1. Mainwaring (1838), *Annals of Bath*
2. Bath Preservation Trust, 1987
3. Chapman, 2010
4. Elliott, 2019, p.123
5. Bath Record Office archives
6. Neale, 1981
7. Save Britain's Heritage, 1982, p.1
8. *Daily Advertiser*, 13th July 1744
9. Parr, 2011, p.44
10. Bath Preservation Trust, 1987
11. Ferguson Mann Architects (2012), 'Options Appraisal for the Cleveland Pools Trust'
12. *Cotswold Archaeology* (2016), 'Cleveland Pools Bath, Bath & North East Somerset, Written Scheme of Investigation for an Archaeological Watching Brief on a Standing Building'. Published by Cotswold Archaeology
13. Bath Preservation Trust, 1987
14. Ensom, A. (2012), 'Conservation Statement', Cleveland Pools, Bath
15. *Bath Chronicle & Weekly Gazette*, 24th April 1817
16. Orme, 1983

Chapter 3
1. *Bath Chronicle and Weekly Gazette*, 20th July 1815
2. E.g., Gyes Directory 1819
3. *Bath Weekly Chronicle*, 24th April 1817
4. Bath Record Office archives
5. *Bath Chronicle*, 12th July 1804

Chapter 4
1. Ancestry.co.uk website
2. *Bath Chronicle and Weekly Gazette*, 5th September 1833
3. Extract from the Duke of Cleveland's Trust Case – Cleveland Baths – Opinion of Mr Brickdale, 28th Nov 1861, Bath Record Office
4. 1841 Census
5. UK City and County Directories 1776–1846
6. *Bath Chronicle and Weekly Gazette*, 1 July 1830
7. London Gazette, Part 1, p.1241
8. Bath Record Office
9. Bath Rates Book, 1828, Bath Record Office
10. *Bath Chronicle and Weekly Gazette*, 3rd March 1836
11. *Bristol Times and Mirror*, 6th May 1840
12. *Gentleman's Magazine*, February 1839
13. *Bath Chronicle and Weekly Gazette*, 10th January 1850
14. 1841 Census
15. 1851 Census
16. *Bath Chronicle and Weekly Gazette*, 10th January 1850
17. *Bath Chronicle and Weekly Gazette*, 30th May 1850
18. *Bath Chronicle and Weekly Gazette*, 3rd August 1854
19. Davenport, P., 2016 Archaeological Watching Brief, Cotswold Archaeology
20. *Bath Chronicle and Weekly Gazette*, 31st December 1857
21. *Bath Chronicle and Weekly Gazette*, 28th December 1858
22. *Bath Chronicle and Weekly Gazette*, 8th July 1858
23. *Bath Chronicle and Weekly Gazette*, 6th January 1859
24. Ensom, A., Cleveland Pools Conservation Statement, 2012
25. *Bath Chronicle and Weekly Gazette*, 8th Feb 1866
26. Bath Miscellanies, 1864
27. *Bath Chronicle and Weekly Gazette*, 17th December 1885
28. *Bath Chronicle and Weekly Gazette*, 26th March 1885
29. *Bath Chronicle and Weekly Gazette*, 26th May 1887
30. *Bath Chronicle and Weekly Gazette*, 20th September 1888
31. *Bell's Life in London and Sporting Chronicle*, 1861, p.6

Chapter 5
1. *Devizes and Wiltshire Gazette*, 15th September 1853
2. *Bath Chronicle and Weekly Gazette*, 8th July 1858
3. *Bath Chronicle and Weekly Gazette*, 4th September 1856
4. *Bath Chronicle and Weekly Gazette*, 22nd August 1861
5. *Bath Chronicle and Weekly Gazette*, 8th September 1934
6. *Bath Chronicle and Weekly Gazette*, 26th August 1869
7. *Bath Chronicle and Weekly Gazette*, 26th August 1869
8. *Bath Chronicle and Weekly Gazette*, 13th May 1869

9. *Bath Chronicle and Weekly Gazette*, 8th September 1934
10. *Western Daily Press*, 25th August 1864
11. *Bath Chronicle and Weekly Gazette*, 22nd November 1894
12. *Bath Chronicle and Weekly Gazette*, 22nd November 1894
13. *Bath Chronicle and Weekly Gazette*, 8th September 1934
14. *Western Daily Press*, 25th August 1864
15. Western Daily Press, 25 August 1864
16. *Bath Chronicle and Weekly Gazette*, 2nd August 1877
17. Bath Record Office, BC/13/8/16
18. Bath Record Office, extract from meeting record, Guildhall, Bath, 15 August 1867
19. Bath Record Office, extract from meeting record, Guildhall, Bath, 23 August 1867
20. *Bath Chronicle and Weekly Gazette*, 20th August 1874
21. *Bath Chronicle and Weekly Gazette*, 22nd July 1880
22. *Bath Chronicle and Weekly Gazette*, 29th July 1880
23. *Bath Chronicle and Weekly Gazette*, 29th July 1880
24. *Bath Chronicle and Weekly Gazette*, 17th August 1882
25. *Bath Chronicle and Weekly Gazette*, 8th September 1934
26. Will of William Evans, Bath Record Office archives
27. *Bath Chronicle and Weekly Gazette*, 8th September 1934
28. *Bath Chronicle and Weekly Gazette*, 17th December 1885
29. *Western Daily Press*, 25th March 1885
30. *Bath Chronicle and Weekly Gazette*, 22nd November 1894
31. *Bath Chronicle and Weekly Gazette*, 29th July 1897
32. Guardian Archive, from *The Guardian*, 24th July 1930

Chapter 6
1. *Bath Chronicle and Weekly Gazette*, 25th October 1900
2. *Bath Chronicle and Weekly Gazette*, 2nd May 1901
3. *Bath Chronicle and Weekly Gazette*, 2nd May 1901
4. *Bath Chronicle and Weekly Gazette*, 2nd May 1901
5. Bath Record Office
6. Obituary, *Bath Chronicle and Weekly Gazette*, 12th October 1915
7. Obituary, *Bath Chronicle and Weekly Gazette*, 12th October 1915
8. *Bath Chronicle and Weekly Gazette*, 8th August 1901
9. Website of the Bath Dolphin Swimming Club
10. *Bath Chronicle and Weekly Gazette*, 11th December 1902
11. *Bath Chronicle and Weekly Gazette*, 15th May 1902
12. *Bath Chronicle and Weekly Gazette*, 11th December 1902
13. *Bath Chronicle and Weekly Gazette*, 20th April 1905
14. *Bath Chronicle and Weekly Gazette*, 25th July 1914
15. *Bath Chronicle and Weekly Gazette*, 10th December 1909
16. *Bath Chronicle and Weekly Gazette*, 16th December 1911
17. *Bath Chronicle and Weekly Gazette*, 4th May 1911
18. *Bath Chronicle and Weekly Gazette*, 4th May 1911
19. *Bath Chronicle and Weekly Gazette*, 9th August 1919
20. Bath Record Office
21. Bath Record Office
22. *Bath Chronicle and Weekly Gazette*, 26th June 1915
23. *Bath Chronicle and Weekly Gazette*, 12th February 1916
24. *Bath Chronicle and Weekly Gazette*, 18th April 1936

25. *Bath Chronicle and Weekly Gazette*, 18th November 1916
26. *Bath Chronicle and Weekly Gazette*, 22nd September 1917
27. *Bath Chronicle and Weekly Gazette*, 8th April 1916
28. *Bath Chronicle and Weekly Gazette*, 16th August 1919
29. *Bath Chronicle and Weekly Gazette*, 12th June 1920
30. *Bath Chronicle and Weekly Gazette*, 15th January 1921

Chapter 7
1. *Bell's Life in London and Sporting Chronicle* (1861), 'Treatise on swimming VI', 24th Feb, p.6
2. *Bath Chronicle and Weekly Gazette*, 24th July 1920
3. *Bath Chronicle and Weekly Gazette*, 31st July 1920
4. *Bath Chronicle and Weekly Gazette*, 15th October 1921
5. *Bath Chronicle and Weekly Gazette*, 28th April 1923
6. *Bath Chronicle and Weekly Gazette*, 14th January1928
7. *Municipal Journal*, 1929
8. *Bath Chronicle and Herald*, 4th February 1933
9. *Bath Chronicle and Weekly Gazette*, 14th February 1920.
10. *Bath Chronicle and Weekly Gazette*, 20th June 1925
11. *Bath Chronicle and Weekly Gazette*, 2nd May 1925
12. 'An overview of the development of swimming in England c1750–1918', *The International Journal of the History of Sport*, 24:5, 2007, pp.568-85
13. 'Local aquatic empires; the municipal provision of swimming pools in England 1828–1918, *The International Journal of the History of Sport*, 2007 24:5 pp.620-89
14. Horwood, C. (2000) 'Girls who arouse dangerous passions: women and bathing, 1900–1939', *Women's History Review*, 9(4), pp.653-73.

Chapter 8
1. *Bath Chronicle and Weekly Gazette*, 28th June 1941
2. *Bath Chronicle and Weekly Gazette*, 28th June 1941
3. Ex-swimmer interviewed by Sally Helvey at the Avondown House Care Home, Bath
4. Ex-swimmer interviewed by Sally Helvey at the Avondown House Care Home, Bath
5. *Bath Chronicle and Weekly Gazette*, 28th June 1941
6. *Bath Chronicle and Weekly Gazette*, 27th July 1940
7. *Bath Chronicle and Weekly Gazette*, 27th July 1940
8. *Bath Chronicle and Weekly Gazette*, 21st December 1940
9. *Bath Chronicle and Weekly Gazette*, 21st December 1940
10. *Bath Chronicle and Weekly Gazette*, 30th May 1942
11. *Bath Chronicle and Weekly Gazette*, 4th July 1942
12. *Bath Chronicle and Weekly Gazette*, 8th September 1945
13. *Central Somerset Gazette*, 21st August 1959
14. Greenbank Pool website
15. *Bath Chronicle and Weekly Gazette*, 28th May 1945
16. *Twerton and Whiteway News*, 1st April 2016
17. Bath Record Office
18. *Bath Chronicle and Weekly Gazette*, 23rd July 1949
19. *Bath Chronicle and Weekly Gazette*, 15th April 1950
20. *Bath Chronicle and Weekly Gazette*, 29th May 1950
21. *Bath Chronicle and Weekly Gazette*, 17th June 1950
22. *Bath Chronicle and Weekly Gazette*, 27th August 1957

Chapter 9

1. Interview carried out by Sally Helvey for the Cleveland Pools Trust
2. Interview carried out by Sally Helvey for the Cleveland Pools Trust
3. Interview carried out by Sally Helvey for the Cleveland Pools Trust at a Cleveland Pools Swimmers' Reunion
4. Interview carried out by Bath Spa University student for the Cleveland Pools Trust
5. *Bath Chronicle and Weekly Gazette*, 14th June 1957
6. *Bath Chronicle and Weekly Gazette*, 10th July 1964
7. Bath City Council record 7th April 1964, Bath Record Office
8. Oestriecher, L. (2016), Historic Architectural Paint Report, Cleveland Pools
9. Bath Record Office
10. *Bath Chronicle and Weekly Gazette*, 23rd July 1949
11. Report to the Spa Committee from the Town Clerk, 5th December 1966, Bath Record Office
12. Bath Record Office

Chapter 10

1. Quote from transcript of Mick Ringham's memories of swimming at the Baths, courtesy of Bath Spa University
2. Blog on the BBC West website, 26th July 2016
3. Blog on the BBC West website, 26th July 2016
4. Quote from transcript of Mick Ringham's memories of swimming at the Baths, courtesy of Bath Spa University
5. Quote from transcript of Richard and Debbie Mower's memories of swimming at the Baths, courtesy of Bath Spa University
6. Quote from transcript of Richard and Debbie Mower's memories of swimming at the Baths, courtesy of Bath Spa University
7. Quote from transcript of Brian Popay's memories of swimming at the Baths, courtesy of Bath Spa University
8. Quotes and information on John Dagger in this chapter included courtesy of John Dagger

Chapter 11

1. Acanthus Ferguson Mann (2006), Cleveland Pools Feasibility Study
2. Bath & North East Somerset Council (2004) information pack: Prospective Sale of the Cleveland Baths
3. English Heritage Grade II* Listing; Summary of Importance, 30th January 2008
4. Ensom, A. (2012), Conservation Statement, The Cleveland Baths, Hampton Row, Bath
5. Davenport, P. (2005), Cleveland Baths, Bathwick, Bath. A standing building assessment, Bath Archaeological Trust.
6. *The Economist* (2017), 'The revival of the great British lido'. Available at: https://www.economist.com/prospero/2017/07/26/the-revival-of-the-great-british-lido (Accessed September 2019)

Acknowledgements

Significant research contributions to the content of this book were made by volunteers Jill Coles, Gillian Clarke, Janice Dreisbach(who sadly died in 2020), Ainslie Ensom, Sally Helvey and Linda Watts. Other research contributions were made by Phil Bendall, Dr Amy Frost, Dr Julie Kent, Mike Macklin, Nicola McNee, Lucy Miller, Dr Michael Rowe and Mary Stacey. Sally Helvey's contribution has included a range of video interviews with previous swimmers.

Beth Swain, an MA Heritage Management student at Bath Spa University, dedicated a course placement in 2019 to research in the Bath Record Office and to carry out a literature review. History students at the University have recorded interviews with ex-swimmers; the consistent partnership approach of Bath Spa University over the last decade is much appreciated.

The Bath Record Office and Bath Central Library have been very helpful to a succession of enthusiastic research volunteers.

The Cleveland Pools Trust thanks those people who contributed their memories of swimming in the Cleveland Baths: Stephanie Adams, Ivor Gibbs, Sue Lucy, Carol Morley, Richard and Debbie Mower, Terry Mitchell, Brian Popay, Mick Ringham, Jean Russell, Derek Stone, Jenny Wyatt, Jack Sparrow and Sheila Stevens. Special thanks to John Dagger, aged 84 in 2020, the last swimming instructor and manager of the Cleveland Baths before they closed in the 1980s.

Long-standing trustees, volunteers and supporters gave accounts of their involvement with the campaign to restore the Pools; they are: Sarah Ball, Tom Boden, Ann Dunlop, Ainslie Ensom, Rob Harding, Ina Harris, Roger Houghton, Ros Kerslake and Trevor Osborne.

June Hannam, Emeritus Professor of History and a Patron of the Cleveland Pools, provided extensive editorial input and guidance, especially relating to the coherence of the narrative. Copyediting and advice has been provided by Katie Crous. Gillian Clarke, Ann Dunlop, Ina and Michael Harris, Roger Houghton and my husband Michael Tichelar helpfully commented on draft chapters, and Paul Simons, Chair of the Cleveland Pools Trustee Board has given supportive advice. Mary Stacey and Tim Graham provided key advice on publishing and useful contacts. Matthew Croft has contributed design input to the cover of this book. Donald Insall Associates, the architects for the Cleveland Pools restoration, have kindly provided a sponsorship grant.

Last but certainly not least, the support and patience of Neil Parkhouse, publisher of Lightmoor Books, has been particularly valued.

Linda Watts,
Research Adviser for the Cleveland Pools Trust

Bibliography

Ayriss, C. (2012). *Hung Out to Dry: Swimming and British Culture.* Self-published: Lulu.com.

Barton, I. (2007). *Sandford Parks Lido: Our History and Community.* Cheltenham: Barton Media.

Bath Preservation Trust (1987). *Beyond Mr Pulteney's Bridge.* Bath: Bath Preservation Trust.

Bathwick Local History Society (2004). *Bathwick: A Forgotten Village.* Bath: Bathwick Local History Society.

Bathwick Local History Society (2008). *Bathwick: Echoes of the Past.* Bath: Bathwick Local History Society.

Birkinshaw, J. (2018). *Celebrating Portishead Open Air Pool.* Clevedon: Clevedon Community Press.

Borsay, P. (1989). 'Image and Counter-Image in Georgian Bath'. *British Journal for Eighteenth Century Studies* 17/1994, pp.165–79.

Borsay, P. (2000). *The Image of Georgian Bath: Towns, Heritage and History.* New York: Oxford University Press.

Byrde, P. (1987). '"That frightful unbecoming dress": clothes for spa bathing at Bath.' Costume, 21(1), pp.50–55.

Campbell, A. (1918). *Report on public baths and wash-houses in the United Kingdom.* Edinburgh: Edinburgh University Press.

Chaline, E. (2017). *Strokes of Genius: A History of Swimming.* London: Reaktion Books.

Chapman, M. (2003). *The Lost Streams of Bath.* Bath: Published for the Survey of Old Bath.

Chapman, M. (2010). *Kensington Meadows Local Nature Reserve Bath: A Desk Based Historical Assessment.* Digitally retrieved via link on Kensington Meadows page of the website of Bath & North East Somerset Council.

Clarke, J. & Critcher, C. (1985). *The Devil Makes Work: Leisure in Capitalist Britain.* London: Macmillan.

Crebbin-Bailey, J., Harcup, J. & Harrington, J. (2004). *The Spa Book.* London: Thomson.

Cregan-Reid, V. (2004). 'Water Defences: The Arts of Swimming in Nineteenth Century Culture'. *Critical Survey* 16 (3) pp.33–47.

Currie, J. (1797). *Medical reports on the effects of water, cold and warm, as a remedy in fever, and febrile diseases.* London: Cadell and Davies. Retrieved digitally from the James Lind Library.

Davis, G. (2009). *Bath as Spa and Bath as Slum.* Lampeter: Edwin Mellen Press.

Davis, G. & Bonsall, P. (1996). *Bath: A New History.* Staffordshire: Keele University Press.

Davis, G. & Bonsall, P. (2006). *A History of Bath: Image and Reality.* Lancaster: Carnegie Publishing.

Digby, E. (1587). *De Arte Natandi.* London: Thomas Dawson. Retrieved digitally from the Wellcome Collection Library.

Doughan, D. & Gordon, P. (2006). *Women, Clubs and Associations in Britain.* Abingdon: Routledge.

Dreisbach, J. (2008). *The Cleveland Pleasure Pools Bath, A Short History.* Bath: Cleveland Pools Trust.

Elliott, K. (2019). *No Swinging on Sundays: The Story of Bath's Lost Pleasure Gardens.* Bath: Akeman Press.

Fawcett, T. (2001). *Bath Administer'd: Corporation Affairs at the 18th Century Spa.* London: Ruton.

Fawcett, T. (2014). *Bath City Council Members 1700–1835.* Bath: History of Bath Research Group.

Floyer, J.S. & Baynard, E. (1715). *Psychrolousia, or, the history of cold bathing: both ancient and modern. In two parts. The first written by Sir John Floyer, the second by Dr Edward Baynard.* London: William Innys. Retrieved digitally from European Libraries.

Gordon, I. & Inglis, S. (2009). *Great Lengths: The historic indoor swimming pools of Britain.* London: English Heritage and Played in Britain.

Gye, F. (1819). *Gye's Bath Directory 1819.* Bath: F. Gye.

Hardick, T. (2005). *Bath Boating Station: An Illustrated History.* Bath: Millstream Books.

Hembry, P. (1997). *British Spas from 1815 to the Present: A Social History.* Edited by L.W. Cowie & E.E. Cowie. London: The Athlone Press.

Horwood, C. (2000). 'Girls who arouse dangerous passions: women and bathing, 1900–1939'. *Women's History Review* 9 (4) pp.653–73.

Jackson, R. (1808). *An Exposition of the Practice of Effusing Cold Water on the Surface of the Body*. Edinburgh: Abernethy and Walker. Retrieved digitally from Google Books.

Jay, C. (1859). *Recollections of William Jay of Bath*. London: Hamilton, Adams & Co. Retrieved digitally from Google Books.

Kilby, P. (2019). *A–Z of Bath: Places – People – History*. Stroud: Amberley Publishing.

Knight, R. (2013). *Britain Against Napoleon: The Organisation of Victory 1793–1815*. London: Penguin.

Kynaston, D. (2009). *Family Britain 1951–57*. London: Bloomsbury Publishing.

Landreth, J. (2017). *Swell: A Waterbiography*. London: Bloomsbury Publishing.

Langhamer, C. (2009). *Women's Leisure in England 1920–1960*. Manchester: Manchester University Press.

Love, C. (2015). *A Social History of Swimming in England 1800–1918: Splashing in the Serpentine*. Abingdon: Routledge.

Lykke Syse, K.V. (2010). 'Ideas of leisure, pleasure and the river in early modern England' in Lykke Syse, K.V. &

Oestigaard, T. (eds) *Perceptions of Water in Britain from Early Modern Times to the Present: An Introduction*. pp.35–57. Bergen: University of Bergen.

Mainwaring, R. (1838). *Annals of Bath: From the Year 1800 to the Passing of the New Municipal Act*. Bath: Mary Meyler & Son.

Marland, H. & Adams, J. (2009). 'Hydropathy at home: the water cure and domestic healing in mid-nineteenth century Britain', *Bulletin of the History of Medicine*, 83(3), pp.499–529.

McCrone, K. (1988). *Playing the Game: Sports and the Physical Emancipation of English Women 1870–1914*. Kentucky: University Press of Kentucky.

McKendrick, N., Brewer, J. & Plumb, J.H. (1982). *The Birth of a Consumer Society: The Commercialization of Eighteenth-Century England. Bloomington*, US: Indiana University Press.

Neale, R.S. (1981). *1680–1850 Bath: A Valley of Pleasure Yet a Sink of Iniquity*. Boston: Routledge and Kegan Paul.

Norton, E. (1850). *Bath Annual Directory*. Bath: Charles Clark.

Orme, N. (1983). *Early British Swimming: 55 BC–AD 1719*. Exeter: University of Exeter Press.

Parr, S. (2011). *The Story of Swimming*. Stockport: Daniel Lewis Media.

Porter, R. (2000). *London: A Social History*. London: Penguin.

Reid, T. (1795). *Directions for Warm and Cold Sea Bathing with Directions on their Applications and Effects in Different Diseases*. Retrieved digitally from Gale ECCO online archive.

Save Britain's Heritage (1982). *Taking the Plunge: The Architecture of Bathing*. London: Save Britain's Heritage.

Sheard, S. (2000). 'Profit is a dirty word: the development of public baths and wash-houses in Britain 1847–1915.' *Social History of Medicine*, 13(1), pp.63–86.

Sherr, L. (2012). *Swim: Why We Love the Water*. New York: Public Affairs.

Smith, J. (2005). *Liquid Assets: The Lidos and Open-Air Swimming Pools of Britain*. Swindon: English Heritage.

Strutt, J. (1801). *Sports and pastimes of the people of England from the earliest period including the rural and domestic recreations, May games, mummeries, pageants, processions and pompous spectacles*. Revised Edition. London: Methuen & Co.

Tomory, L. (2017). *The History of the London Water Industry, 1580–1820*. Maryland, US: John Hopkins *University Press*.

Wesley, J. (1747). *Primitive Physick, or, an Easy and Natural Method of Curing Most Diseases*. Revised Edition. Edinburgh: Thornton & Collie.

Index

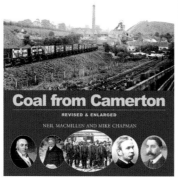
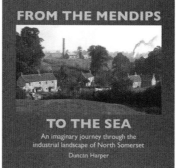
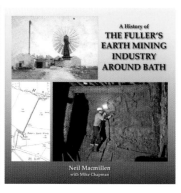
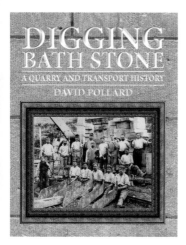
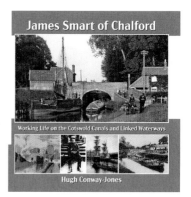
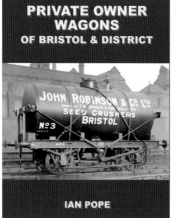

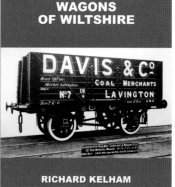